Gwladys Street's
Holy Trinity
Kendall, Harvey & Ball

David France & Becky Tallentire

'The Holy Trinity' title was borrowed from Brian Labone.
The sub-title wording proved to be far more challenging and different permutations of the three names were considered. Because no consensus could be reached on the criteria to be used, such as alphabetical order, duration of club service, collection of England caps, popularity with the Goodison faithful or sequence of shirt numbers, it was decided to adopt the arbitrary approach of listing the three Evertonians by height - in descending order. Hence the book title: *Gwladys Street's Holy Trinity - Kendall, Harvey & Ball.*

Howard Kendall, Colin Harvey and Alan Ball ... their royal blue names simply roll off the tongue. What terrific players! What a superb midfield unit!

As a veteran of more than 500 appearances, I was honoured to be a member of several Everton teams who successfully reinforced the School of Science's reputation for fast and flowing football in the post-war years. During my time at the club we had our fair share of outstanding athletes and perhaps more than our share of great characters. Many were super-stars with international reputations. Some like Dave Hickson - 'The Cannonball Kid', Bobby Collins - 'The Little General' and Alex Young - 'The Golden Vision' were a little bit special and captured the hearts of the Goodison faithful. But for me, no period was more exciting than the glorious reign of Kendall, Harvey & Ball.

Masterminded by Harry Catterick and driven by the rolling thunder of this midfield trio, our young team played with a cultured style of unparalleled quality. Their sublime ball skills, sharp passing, strong tackling, adroit positioning, superior stamina combined with never-say-die enthusiasm made every contest enjoyable. Although we did not go undefeated at Goodison, we did kick off every game with the genuine belief that we were better equipped for battle than our opponents. A confidence derived from the advantage of fielding such talented footballers across the middle of the park. Of course, we were much more than a three-man outfit and boasted established England internationals like West, Wright, Newton, Wilson and Royle as well as unsung heroes such as Brown, Hurst, Husband, Jackson, Kenyon, Whittle and Morrissey. But it was our talented midfield trio who caught the imaginations of the football enthusiasts as they out-thought, out-fought and out-ran their opponents.

Like other Evertonians, I had expected that the combined talents of Kendall, Harvey & Ball would have enabled us to compete for the highest honours in England and Europe for many seasons. I was as surprised as anyone when the team which had been so dominant during the 69/70 championship campaign began to struggle against quite modest opposition. Since then I have tried to rationalise our dramatic change in fortunes, but the decline and eventual break up of such a young team with so much quality and even more unrealised potential remains somewhat of a mystery to me. Clearly we were hampered by a series of injuries to key members of the team and by the demands of defending the World Cup in 1970. Nevertheless, the talents of Kendall, Harvey & Ball deserved far greater rewards than one Division 1 crown and one FA Cup final appearance. They should be remembered as the most dominant midfield unit ever fielded by a British club.

I retired from football in 1972, shortly after Alan Ball had departed to Highbury, but those great days in blue and white playing alongside Howard, Colin and Bally are etched in my memory forever. It is a privilege for me to be associated with this tribute to the only three-man team to have ever won the League championship.

Kendall, Harvey & Ball were sent to Goodison from heaven - they were 'The Holy Trinity' of the beautiful game.

Brian Labone

𝔉𝔬𝔯𝔢𝔴𝔬𝔯𝔡 𝔟𝔶 𝔅𝔯𝔦𝔞𝔫 𝔏𝔞𝔟𝔬𝔫𝔢

Kendall, Harvey & Ball

It is only once in a generation that the gods of football provide the ideal formula for the beautiful game. In the late-sixties, the followers of the royal blue faith were convinced that Goodison Park had been duly blessed - with the presence of Howard Kendall, Colin Harvey and Alan Ball.

Respected as outstanding footballers in their own rights in an era of exceptional British players, the union of Kendall, Harvey & Ball represented the most stylish midfield unit ever assembled by a British club. Their repertoire of skills and telepathic understanding was beyond belief. Perhaps their special chemistry was a product of meticulous planning by the Goodison hierarchy or simply good fortune. No matter what the reason, their special blend of vision, technique, guile, courage and industry, thrilled football purists of all persuasions with breath-taking displays of the beautiful game. Such tributes may sound like hyperbole and the three young Englishmen may sound like fantasy footballers - but the fans who witnessed them in the sixties can confirm that 'The Holy Trinity' was indeed a revelation.

For those who do not believe in divine intervention, the Kendall, Harvey & Ball story was masterminded by Everton chairman John Moores. He had recruited Harry Catterick in 1960 to enhance the curriculum at the School of Science. The manager's inheritance included established stars such as Alex Young, Roy Vernon, Bobby Collins and Jimmy Gabriel as well as several promising local lads. Although most of these youngsters were to slip into obscurity, one inside-left was to make a lasting impression - Colin Harvey.

The new boss immediately set about strengthening his first-team with players familiar to him. He fine-tuned the engine room by recruiting Dennis Stevens and galvanised the defence with Gordon West and Ramon Wilson. He then added midfield dynamo Tony Kay from his former club Sheffield Wednesday and Everton carried off the Division 1 title in 1962/63 with ease. Nevertheless Catterick sought to build his own team. His blueprint employed Tony Kay as the nucleus and emphasised graduates from the club's youth development programme, however, his plans were derailed in 1965 when Kay was banned from football for life. As a consequence, Catterick was forced to search elsewhere for that special catalyst. During this transitional period Everton lifted the FA Cup and, perhaps more importantly in the manager's eyes, he identified the prerequisite for his dream team. Heading his short-list was - Alan Ball. England's World Cup hero had been courted by Don Revie and appeared destined to team up with Billy Bremner and Johnny Giles at Leeds. Catterick's vigilance paid off and a British record fee ensured that the midfielder joined Everton at the start of the 66/67 season. Although the club's fortunes benefited significantly from Ball's arrival, Catterick believed that something was still missing from his formula for perfect chemistry. He remedied the situation six months later by persuading another much sought-after youngster to join Everton in preference to their red neighbours. He was - Howard Kendall.

Catterick's strategy of only targeting the outstanding players on his wish-list was to pay handsome dividends and few on Merseyside would dispute that the honed midfield triumvirate dominated English football during their heyday. 'The Toffee Triangle' excelled against their most accomplished adversaries such as Bremner & Giles, MacKay & Gemmill at Derby and Stiles & Crerand at Old Trafford and over one million members of the royal blue faithful worshipped annually at their Goodison shrine. But to others, they remained something of an enigma and their talents were not heralded throughout the land. Perhaps their reign was too fleeting, their accomplishments too modest or their geographic location unfashionable. Although Ball was widely respected as a mainstay in the England camp, Harvey received only one England cap and the claims of Kendall were ignored completely. In fact to defend the Jules Rimet trophy in 1970, Sir Alf Ramsey selected four players from Everton but left behind both Harvey and Kendall.

As British football basked in the after-glow of England winning the World Cup and Celtic capturing the European Cup, Catterick's colts gained the prerequisite experience for their championship assault. After flirting with the FA Cup in 1967, 1968 and 1969, they romped away with the Division 1 title in 1970. Everton, with an average age of 23 years, were widely tipped to carry off more glistening prizes and to rule Europe for many years. Indeed Kendall, Harvey & Ball appeared to be on the threshold of invincibility but failed to accumulate the honours that their special chemistry merited.

Since their final game together on December 4, 1971, many fans have questioned why their tenure at the zenith of the game was so short-lived. One popular belief is that Ball and his World Cup team-mates never recovered fully from the frustrations of allowing the trophy to slip from their grasp in Mexico. Another is that Catterick's disciplinarian approach was less effective with seasoned professionals than malleable youngsters. Also a catalogue of injuries impacted team selection. Whatever the reasons the champions failed to regain their rhythm and their fall from grace was effectively sealed when they were eliminated from the latter stages of the European Cup by Greek underdogs and the FA Cup by their red shadows. As a consequence, paradise was postponed and the balance of Merseyside power dramatically swung towards Anfield.

Although the club was respected as 'The Merseyside Millionaires', commercial considerations were to further blacken the Goodison skies when Ball was sold to Arsenal - albeit for a record fee of £220,000. The Everton directors boasted that the sale made good business sense and cited a 100% profit. The Goodison faithful were less convinced. Whatever the real reasons behind Ball's defection, the speed of the transaction only served to fuel the rumour mill and send unsettling repercussions throughout the club. As Catterick toiled in vain to attract a new midfield maestro to fill the famous white boots, he suffered a heart attack and team performances deteriorated further in his absence. The decline was exacerbated by the unavailability of Harvey because of eye and hip injuries and Kendall was required to soldier on with an assortment of midfield partners including big-money acquisitions like Mike Bernard and promising youngsters like Mick Buckley. Predictably Billy Bingham, the new manager, sought to build his own team and brought the curtain down in 1974 by disposing of both Howard Kendall and Colin Harvey.

The royal blue faithful as well as many other fans of the beautiful game were to discover that 'The Holy Trinity' were irreplaceable. Although they managed only 140 games together, their classical style of football is revered as much today as it was during their heyday. This book celebrates their accomplishments and also attempts to illuminate many of the nagging questions associated with the exciting, but sadly all too transient, reign of Kendall, Harvey & Ball. To this end, we have published extracts from interviews with nearly 200 individuals who knew them best - their team-mates and their fans. Many of their recollections are candid.

David France

Becky Tallentire

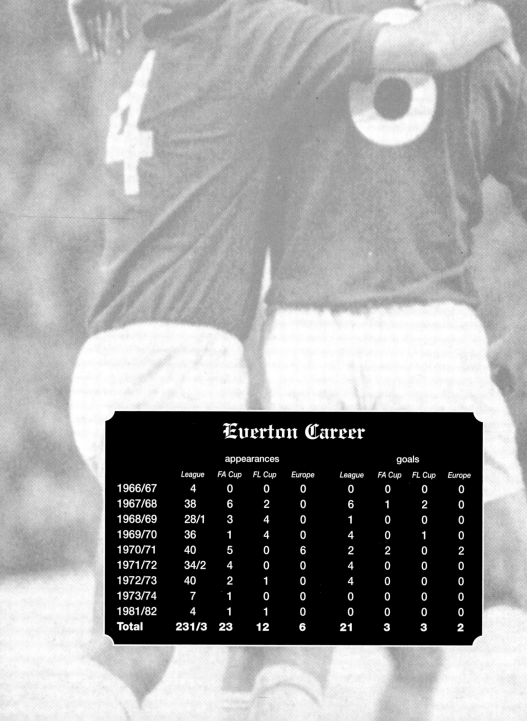

Everton Career

	appearances				goals			
	League	FA Cup	FL Cup	Europe	League	FA Cup	FL Cup	Europe
1966/67	4	0	0	0	0	0	0	0
1967/68	38	6	2	0	6	1	2	0
1968/69	28/1	3	4	0	1	0	0	0
1969/70	36	1	4	0	4	0	1	0
1970/71	40	5	0	6	2	2	0	2
1971/72	34/2	4	0	0	4	0	0	0
1972/73	40	2	1	0	4	0	0	0
1973/74	7	1	0	0	0	0	0	0
1981/82	4	1	1	0	0	0	0	0
Total	**231/3**	**23**	**12**	**6**	**21**	**3**	**3**	**2**

Howard Kendall

observations of his team-mates

HOWARD KENDALL

He was the youngest player
to appear in an FA Cup final
when he represented
Preston North End in 1964.

A decade later his label was
changed to the finest player
never to have won full
international honours.

League Career

		appearances	goals
Preston North End	1962/63-66/67	104	13
Everton	1966/67-73/74	227/3	22
Birmingham City	1973/74-76/77	115	16
Stoke City	1977/78-78/79	82	9
Blackburn Rovers	1979/80-80/81	79	6
Everton	1981/82	4	1

When are you going to start playing for us ...

I was born the son of a coal-miner but was destined to become a professional footballer. My progress was quite spectacular - I left grammar school to join Preston North End as a 15-year old apprentice and became the youngest player to appear in an FA Cup final two years later. But with Preston languishing in Division 2, I eventually sought greater opportunities elsewhere. My chance to join the big time came when Jimmy Milne, the manager at Deepdale, turned up on our doorstep and announced that a big club had come in for me. The local press had speculated that it would be Liverpool or Tottenham - but it was neither, it was Everton.

I don't know if Harry Catterick was worried about another club making a late bid but he was waiting for me at Deepdale and I arranged to travel down to Merseyside in my red MG sports car. The Everton manager took one look at my pride and joy: *"Either get it sprayed or prepare for the worst. You have no idea what they're like down here."* Stoke City came in with an eleventh hour bid and offered better terms. Alan Ball Senior was working for them at the time and my dad and I met him to discuss my prospects at the Victoria Ground. My father asked him: *"Why are you trying to get our Howard to sign for Stoke when your own son is enjoying so much success at Goodison Park."* I don't remember his response but it must not have been convincing because shortly afterwards I joined Everton and swapped my car for a blue model.

At £80,000, the transfer was a big price-tag for a 20-year old, and after completing the paperwork Harry Catterick took me to one side and said *"Welcome to the big time!"* His words were ringing in my ears as I entered the dressing room at the Bellefield training ground for the first time and looked around - there was Alan Ball, Alex Young, Ray Wilson and company. Unfortunately, my start was hardly auspicious. Sometimes that's not such a bad thing because it stops you becoming big headed, but I was overawed on my Goodison debut against Southampton. It was a nightmare of leaden legs and, to make matters worse, was one of the few home games that Everton lost that season. I remember driving back to Preston with my father. It was a terrible night, pouring with rain. When we stopped for petrol not far from the ground, I looked over and saw some supporters filling their car. I was distraught with my performance and preferred not to be recognised - I just wanted to get home. But one by one they approached me, knelt down in the puddles in front of the car and bowed. It was absolutely unbelievable. Harry Catterick was right, it was the big time and I so wanted to please these devoted Evertonians.

I like to think that I was a pretty decent one-touch player and also took pride in my abilities to tackle and read the game. I was never someone who could go on mazy runs or lick opponents for pace, but not being the fastest encourages you to think quicker. Catterick had planned for me to replace Jimmy Gabriel but I didn't settle quickly. For a start I was cup-tied and with Everton still involved in the competition, having beaten Liverpool in the fifth round, I don't think that the boss wanted to chop and change the side. I was also handicapped by a niggling knee ligament injury. During this early period I bumped into John Moores in the lift at Goodison: *"You're Kendall aren't you? We've paid a lot of money for you, when are you going to start playing for us?"* His words haunted me for weeks but thankfully things came together at the beginning of the next season. I loved my football at Everton and was blessed to play alongside some incredibly talented individuals.

Howard Kendall

Leicester City   September 30, 1967

Kendall hit the headlines with Preston North End playing for them in the 1964 Cup final when only 17 years 345 days, the youngest ever in a Wembley final. Kendall from Washington, Co. Durham was the target of several clubs when Mr Catterick pipped them by signing him on March 10 at a reported £80,000. Debut on March 19 versus Southampton. Hobbies are hairdressing and organ-playing.

Wolverhampton Wanderers   October 26, 1968

Became the youngest player to appear in the FA Cup final when he was on the losing side with Preston against West Ham in 1964. Yet when he joined Everton to do a man's job with his man's build for the man-sized fee of £80,000 in March 1967, he still was a month short of his twenty-first birthday. Howard, who plays the organ in his spare time, has the immediate ambition of adding a full England cap to those he holds at every other level and the realisation is well within his talents.

Sunderland   February 7, 1970

First jumped into the national headlines when appearing for Preston in the 1964 FA cup final when 17. He was the youngest ever Cup finalist. Transferred to Everton on March 10, 1967 for a then record fee for an under-21 player. His first League appearance was on March 18 and since then he has gained many Under-23 caps though his career has twice been interrupted by injury. He trained throughout the summer to cure an Achilles tendon injury from which he is now completely recovered.

Nottingham Forest   March 20, 1971

Born Washington, Co. Durham, and made a big name as a youngster with Preston North End, for whom he played in the 1964 FA Cup final. Transferred to Everton in March, 1967. Has played for the England Under-23 team, and now ranks with the most stylish players in the country.

Manchester City   October 9, 1971

Has no full cap - yet - and his admirers are mystified about that. He was the youngest player to appear in a Cup final when he played for Preston against West Ham at the age of 17. A big buy in 1967.

Arsenal   September 5, 1972

Captain and distinguished midfield player who reached the headlines in 1964 when, aged 17 years 345 days, he became the youngest-ever FA Cup finalist for Preston against West Ham. Had made his League debut at 16 and signed for Everton in an £80,000 transfer in March 1967. He quickly developed into the England Under-23 side where he made six appearances and has been on the brink of selection for a full cap. Approaching his 200th League appearance for Everton. 5 ft 8 in, 11 st.

Birmingham City   October 27, 1973

Millions of uncommitted fans so much wanted Preston to win the 1964 FA Cup final because Howard, just 17 years 345 days, that day became the youngest player ever to appear in the FA Cup final. Howard, who had first appeared in Preston's team when he was 16, became a regular member of England's Youth XI and it was clear that he was going to be too good a player for Preston to hold. Everton paid £80,000 for his transfer in March 1967, this move enabling him to mature to the point where he was ready for inclusion in the Under-23 team. Howard was on a losing Wembley side again in 1968 when Everton were beaten by an extra-time goal by West Brom. Championship medal: 1970. England Under-23: 6 caps.

Impressions of Howard Kendall ...

Howard Kendall combined masterly tackling and astute positional play with honest endeavour.

Derek Temple: Preston seemed to have a special relationship with Liverpool, having already sold them Gordon Milne, Davie Wilson and Peter Thompson. So we were all surprised when the boss lured Howard from under Bill Shankly's nose. I'd been included as part of the original deal but delayed my move to Deepdale for several months so I'm in the unique position to confirm that Howard was highly respected by the players and the fans at both clubs.

Jimmy Husband: Howard was a very good tackler and had tremendous long-ball distribution. He was the best parts of Graeme Souness and Glenn Hoddle rolled into one - but, of course, not to look at.

Brian Labone: Our ready-made superstar cost £80,000, which was a lot of money in 1967, and was touted as the final piece of Harry Catterick's jigsaw puzzle. It was soon clear to everyone that the boss had made another shrewd investment. I liked Howard. He impressed me as a mature, well-mannered and conscientious 20-year old. He was also a tremendous tackler, a superb passer of the ball and, to cap it off, had a rasping shot. When I think about it, Howard had the lot - except that he had no left foot, but he'd probably dispute that.

Alex Young: Sometimes first impressions can be embarrassingly misleading and I must admit that I wasn't immediately impressed with Howard. He took time to settle but after a few months there was no question in my mind that Harry Catterick had bought another exceptionally talented midfielder. More than anything, Howard was a terrific tackler who had developed the rare knack of coming away with the ball. He was hard but always fair. However there was much more to his game than his strength and courage. Howard possessed great football skills, although he was perhaps the least skilful of the three, and a great football brain.

Roger Kenyon: I'm about three years younger than Howard and was an apprentice when he signed. Straight away I recognised that he was a footballer of rare talent who was mature for his years and had developed a professional approach to the game. This helped him to cope with the spotlight following his big-money move from Preston and his shaky start at Goodison. He was professional in everything that he did. In training, he worked hard at improving his stamina and sharpening his skills and seemed to enjoy his football more than most.

Frank D'arcy: He experienced some difficulty adapting to the pace of the big League but by the middle of the 67/68 season he'd knitted with the other two. Bally always liked to take charge of the dressing room at half-time and would get on his back by complaining: *"Why didn't you cover for me?"* Howard was a very polite and a quiet lad and I got the distinct impression that he was a bit scared of Bally's bark. Sometimes Howard's shoulders would go down and he'd withdraw like a snail. In contrast, Colin would tell Bally to button his lip.

Tommy Wright: Howard was a kind man and an honest player who could be very determined when he wanted to be. These qualities made him a truly outstanding footballer and I don't think he ever got the credit or the recognition that his footballing abilities deserved.

Colin Harvey: It was the start of the 67/68 season when I realised we'd gelled into a very special midfield unit. We seemed to know instinctively where the others were and what they were going to do next. But we weren't clones, in fact we had very different personalities and were different types of footballers. Howard was a truly magnificent footballer in his own right but most of all I admired his unselfishness.

Born: Ryton on Tyne - May 22, 1946
Everton registration date: March 10, 1967
Everton debut: Southampton at Goodison Park on March 18, 1967
Final Everton appearance: Coventry City at Goodison Park on December 28, 1981

Jimmy Gabriel: Howard was young and had more legs than me. He was a very good player and fitted in really well with Colin and Alan. Harry Catterick wanted me to move from midfield to play alongside Brian Labone until John Hurst found his feet, but I wanted to play in midfield. So I moved on to Southampton and handed my treasured No 4 shirt over to Howard, I knew it was in good hands.

Keith Newton: Howard was a player of true international quality and had collected England honours at schoolboy, youth and Under-23 levels. He was desperately unlucky not to have received full-international recognition. Alf Ramsey had told him that he was to make his debut against Yugoslavia and I believe that his family travelled down to Wembley only to discover that Colin Bell had been picked instead. Nevertheless, he had become an integral part of Harry Catterick's plans and Kendall, Harvey & Ball were already the darlings of Goodison by the time I joined Everton. Of course I'd played against him when I was at Blackburn and had been impressed with his skilful game. But it was only during my brief spell on Merseyside that I learned to fully appreciate his commitment to his team-mates and to Everton.

Joe Royle: The tremendous success that Howard enjoyed as a manager will always be a part of Merseyside folklore, so it's sometimes forgotten that he had been a very influential player in his own right - and not only as a part of our great 1970 championship team. People also fail to remember that not long after the glory years of Kendall, Harvey & Ball, he almost single-handedly kept the club away from the relegation trap door.

Steve Seargeant: Howard was the most gilded of the Goodison icons. He was a great pro and an even greater Evertonian who worked hard at improving his game and at sharing his know-how with the club's youngsters. I made my first-team debut about a month after Alan Ball had left for more fertile pastures and was honoured to wear the famous blue and white alongside Kendall and Harvey. We earned a morale-boosting 2-1 win over West Brom that day and I was very much aware that Howard had become the soul of Everton in the absence of Ball. It was a burden that he willingly carried for several seasons. By my next outing in August 1972, the seeds of destruction had been sewn. Only Harvey, Husband, Royle, Wright and, of course, Howard Kendall had survived from the championship side.

Alan Whittle: He was an excellent player with exquisite footballing manners but I don't recall learning much from him. To be honest I thought he was a little naive, he certainly wasn't as worldly as some of the other pros at Bellefield. I was more influenced by the steel of Tony Kay and Johnny Morrissey and the silk of Alex Young.

Tommy Jackson: It was a shame that the famous Kendall, Harvey & Ball combination was broken up because they could have dominated English football for years, sweeping everything in front of them. Howard fought off the threat of Henry Newton's arrival to retain his place in the heart of Everton midfield. He was also a thoughtful leader, something that he confirmed when he retired from playing and went into management.

Brian Labone: Howard has always had a decent sense of humour. I remember that he hadn't been at Everton very long when we had to make the long trek to Portman Road. On the return journey we would take a coach from Ipswich to London and then hop on a train to Lime Street and we never got back before midnight. Howard had arranged to see a friend somewhere in Derbyshire and was to catch a different train out of Euston station. He made the mistake of telling some of the lads that he'd stashed a few bottles of wine in his bag for the weekend. Just before our train departed we distracted him and replaced his refreshments with some sort of ballast. Well, you should have seen his face as our train pulled away from the platform with Westie, Big Joe and Johnny Morrissey toasting him with his own wine.

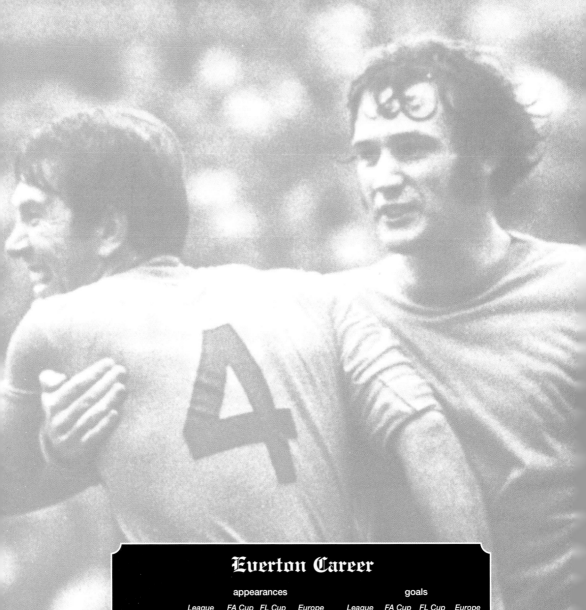

𝕰verton 𝕮areer

	appearances				goals			
	League	FA Cup	FL Cup	Europe	League	FA Cup	FL Cup	Europe
1963/64	2	0	0	1	0	0	0	0
1964/65	32	4	0	4	2	1	0	2
1965/66	40	8	0	4	1	1	0	0
1966/67	42	6	0	4	1	0	0	0
1967/68	34	4	2	0	0	0	0	0
1968/69	36	4	4	0	4	0	0	0
1969/70	35	0	3	0	3	0	0	0
1970/71	36	5	0	6	2	1	0	0
1971/72	17	3	0	0	3	1	0	0
1972/73	24/2	0	1	0	0	0	0	0
1973/74	15/2	0	0/1	0	1	0	0	0
1974/75	4	0	0	0	1	0	0	0
Total	**317/4**	**34**	**10/1**	**7**	**18**	**4**	**0**	**2**

Colin Harvey

observations of his team-mates

JAMES COLIN HARVEY

Born an Evertonian and
baptised at the San Siro,
he illuminated Goodison
with his immaculate ball
skills for over a decade.

The followers of the royal
blue persuasion anointed
him 'The White Pele'.

League Career

		appearances	goals
Everton	1963/64-74/75	317/4	18
Sheffield Wednesday	1974/75-75/76	45	2

Everton was the only team for me ...

My family are Evertonians through-and-through. As a kid I'd watch the match from the boys' pen and would meet my dad afterwards outside the pawn shop on City Road. I was smaller than average and tried to model my own game on Nobby Fielding. Although most of my school-mates were four years older than me, my size didn't prevent me from helping my school to win the Catholic School's Cup. I had a trial at Melwood, but Everton was the only club for me and my uncle rescued me from a fate worse than death by arranging for a trial at Goodison Park, which was held on the practice pitch behind the Park End stand. As a result I played for the C-team on the following Saturday afternoon but, of course, never told them that I'd already turned out for my school that morning. A few weeks later Harry Cooke, the chief scout, met with my parents and was lost for words when he learned that I'd already started my first job earlier that day. That Monday evening I signed apprentice forms with Everton and the next morning had to terminate my career with the National Health Service after just one day. Begrudgingly my boss accepted my decision but insisted that I work two weeks notice. It's the only time in my life that I've had a real job.

Along with Tommy Wright, I progressed through the junior teams. I found training to be the real joy and learned to do the business on match days. My big break came quite literally out of the blue in September 1964. I'd played in a Central League game at Hillsborough and was invited to travel to Milan - as an extra body to help carry the skips or so I thought. Harry Catterick announced his line-up on the morning of the game: *"With Gabby injured, Dennis Stevens will drop back into Gabby's position and Colin Harvey will come in."* I was 18 and about to make my debut in the San Siro!

Of course I was back with the Reserves the next weekend but it's still difficult to comprehend that I played in the Lancashire League and the European Cup during the same year. When I eventually got back into the first-team, some of the crowd gave me a hard time but thankfully Gabby took it upon himself to look after me both on and off the pitch until I found my feet. By 1966 I was ready for bigger challenges like our thrilling fight back in the FA Cup final. We'd been over-run in midfield and I was beginning to think that we'd have to wait another year when two flashes of inspiration from Mike Trebilcock and an unbelievable goal from Derek Temple turned May 14 into a fairy-tale. Although we weren't a particularly good side, we had brought the FA Cup back to Goodison after a wait of 33 years.

By complete contrast, we played some really great football throughout the 69/70 season and had effectively captured the championship by late-March. Alan Whittle got the opener after 20 minutes in the final home game against West Brom and I added the second 10 minutes later. It was a terrific feeling and the Goodison lap of honour brought back memories of the Blues clinching the title in 1963. On that day I'd been playing for the B-team and had shot over to Goodison to watch the last quarter of an hour against Fulham. My own League championship campaign had been a roller-coaster ride. Mid-way through the season I'd been troubled by inflammation on my optic nerve, the treatment involved steroids and took three months to clear up. I re-discovered my fitness during the run-in and eventually broke into the England reckoning only to be sidelined by a niggling hip injury. Years later that problem was diagnosed as an arthritic hip which resulted in two replacement operations. Nevertheless playing for my beloved Everton alongside the likes of Howard and Bally had been a dream come true.

Colin Harvey

Fulham   October 16, 1965

Discovered in pre-season trials. Harvey graduated through the junior teams as an inside-right, and was only 18 when called upon for a most exacting debut. Having become a professional on 24 October 1962, Harvey was brought in to play against Inter Milan, the eventual winners of the European Cup, and came through well. Made League debut on September 14, 1964 against Manchester United and has since missed only three matches.

Sheffield Wednesday at Wembley   May 14, 1966

Pitched into duty against Inter Milan in 1962. A good ball player, but a very useful deliverer of long-distance passes when he's pressed into service in the half-back line. He has the skill to undo most defences but he lacks, at the moment, the confidence to produce the form he shows on the training ground.

West Bromwich Albion at Wembley   May 18, 1968

Another of Everton's former juniors and an England Under-23 cap, Harvey's first appearance was against Inter Milan in the European Cup. Though he came out of that stiff test with flying colours, it was not until the end of that winter that he made his League debut. The following season he established himself as a regular first-team choice at inside forward, switching to the No 6 shirt at the start of the 66/67 campaign.

Burnley   April 8, 1969

Former schoolboy who began as an inside forward. Colin's goal from that position took Everton to Wembley in 1966. Last season completed 150 League appearances and has played in 22 FA Cup ties. An Under-23 player who like several of Everton's young players must be on the short list for the 1970 World Cup.

Chelsea   August 8, 1970

Fine player who was kept out for a spell because of eye trouble, but for which he may have made the World Cup party. Has five Under-23 caps and played for England XI in Mexico on 1969 summer tour. Born Liverpool, 5 ft 7 in, 11 st.

Manchester United   September 2, 1970

Harvey is a player's player, a young man who has always been ready to accept responsibility and who since winning a regular place has chalked up well over 200 First Division appearances, with 35 in the last campaign to earn a Championship medal to add to his Cup winners' medal and five caps at Under-23 level.

Newcastle United   April 25, 1973

Now something of a veteran with the club. Made his debut against Inter Milan in 1963 and has gone on to make over 300 appearances, win a championship medal, a Cup winners' medal and an England cap.

Arsenal   December 22, 1973

Injuries beginning last season have interrupted his brilliant midfield career. Made senior debut in September 1963, and established a first-team place the following season. Joined Everton as a 16-year old, turning professional two years later and has made over 300 League appearances. One full international cap.

Impressions of Colin Harvey ...

Colin Harvey exhibited style in everything that he did, linking it with a colossal work-rate.

Jimmy Husband: Colin Harvey always wanted the ball and had terrific short control. I'm sure that he played with bubble-gum on both boots. In contrast the ball tended to bounce off my feet - but there again I had the pace to catch it up!

Howard Kendall: I had played against Colin in junior football during my days at Preston, but there were so many outstanding youngsters at Everton that I hadn't singled him out. When I moved to Merseyside, it soon became evident that he was a very gifted footballer. Technically - he was absolutely tremendous. I was impressed by his desire to work, but the first thing to hit me was his level of skill - he oozed skill. He was also an awesome athlete and was very friendly with Tommy Wright. One particular morning Tommy wasn't feeling at his best - I think that he'd been out celebrating the christening of Labby's daughter, Rochelle, the night before. As usual, we started with circuits behind the gym, a rigorous routine that required us to train in pairs. When Colin had completed his circuit, Tommy was supposed to do his, but this morning our international full-back hid his sore head behind the Bellefield trees leaving his partner to do both sets of circuits. As always, Colin attacked the first circuit with characteristic enthusiasm, then did the next and the next and so on. Gradually slowing down through exhaustion, he got a real roasting from Wilf Dixon for not keeping up with everyone. But that was Colin - unbelievable in his willingness to work hard and not let anyone down. You get different characters in football and different pain thresholds. Most players carry little injuries, very few are lucky enough to be 100% fit but there is a point when you know that you shouldn't play. Colin so wanted to play for Everton that perhaps he turned out when he shouldn't have. Whether training or playing, he always wanted to do his best for the club that he loved.

Brian Labone: I've seen many stars shine and fade away but even as a young apprentice you could tell that Colin was that bit special. Even so I didn't think that he would break into the first-team as quickly as he did. Colin developed into an influential player in no time. He was so quick, so sharp and so good on the ball that I believe he was one of the few British players who could have made it on the continent. You couldn't get near him to tackle him. He was also a tough character for a little fella but unfortunately couldn't shake off injuries easily when he got clobbered. His only weakness was that he didn't score that many goals. Without question his most important strike was in the semi-final at Burnden and even that one bobbled a bit.

Roger Kenyon: Perhaps more than anything, I was impressed by his intense determination to do his best for his beloved Toffees - the club he'd followed as a kid in Fazakerley. He was Everton-mad and never hid the fact that pulling on the No 6 shirt - be it blue or amber - was very important to him. During his playing days, Colin was ultra-competitive in everything that he did and wanted to win every game - even in training.

Alex Young: Although he was just a wee lad with curly hair, Colin immediately impressed me as a good little player. He was dedicated to pursuing a career in professional football and trained with the apprentices at Bellefield during the first close-season. The extra training made him stronger and I could see a real difference in his sprinting. I'd say that he had increased his pace by a yard or two and had been transformed from someone who could have ended up, like many before him, playing for Southport in a couple of years to someone who was going to make it in the big time. To be honest I'd never seen such a transformation and I knew it wouldn't be long before he broke into the first-team. Sure enough he matured into a buzz bomb of a footballer - an expert at precise and imaginative passing. Play and run, play and run - that was Colin. He was unselfish, really brave and incredibly skilful. But one thing never changed, he was always a nice wee lad with curly hair.

Born: Liverpool - November 16, 1944
Everton registration date: October 24, 1962
Everton debut: Internazionale at San Siro, Milan on September 25, 1963
Final Everton appearance: Arsenal at Goodison Park on August 31, 1974

Tommy Jackson: Colin Harvey was a colossal talent. He was a superb left-sided midfielder who later on in his career picked up a few injuries which ultimately lead to him receiving two hip replacements, a bit like another ageing aristocrat - the Queen Mother!

Alan Ball: Colin looked every inch a footballer. I'd played against him during my early days at Blackpool and was aware of his cultured technique, tremendous work-rate and competitive spirit. But at Everton, he impressed me most with his insatiable willingness to learn. He loved training and never stopped working at trying to improve his game.

Gordon Watson: I was introduced to his footballing skills when I coached the Reserves. It was clear that this 16-year old kid was going to be a very good professional. He had something about him - he looked like a footballer. Because he already had the best passing ability that I'd seen in an apprentice, we concentrated on improving his technique to keep the ball within his playing distance. We practiced for hours after his team-mates had gone home. Colin was a quick learner and I pride myself on knowing that I taught him how to master the ball.

Ray Wilson: Playing in the same side as Colin was a full-back's dream. In my humble opinion, he was the ideal team-mate who possessed plenty of skill and liked to do lots of running. If I was to engrave his head-stone, it would read: *"I liked Colin Harvey - he always tracked back."*

Sandy Brown: I played behind the greatest midfield of all time, Howard Kendall, Alan Ball and the best of the bunch, Colin Harvey. Whereas Ball was a blur of red, white and blue, 'The White Pele' was so classy - he even perspired with style.

Gordon West: Colin was no angel and his sublime ball skills masked a very competitive streak which, even as an apprentice, got him into trouble every now and then. Sending-offs were scarce in the good old days, nevertheless I recall that Colin's over-enthusiasm got him his marching orders for fighting on two occasions. The first time was at Craven Cottage and the other was at Filbert Street a few seasons later, when we were recovering from our post-Wembley blues. Of course, Alan Ball was more notorious for getting on the wrong side of referees but I don't remember him ever getting into a fight, well not with the opposition. Bally did succeed in getting himself sent off against Newcastle at Goodison during the 67/68 season but I think it was for dissent - calling the referee names.

John Hurst: In addition to his abilities to shimmy past opponents and pierce defences with telling passes, Colin was a combative competitor. He loved to patrol the middle of the park with his biting tackles, so much so that we used to call him 'Snarler'.

Tommy Wright: We came through the club's junior teams together, from the C-team to the first-team, and have remained the best of friends. Colin was my room-mate and I'm pleased to report that he didn't have any bad habits. He didn't even snore.

Brian Labone: Many players get pre-match butterflies and this was a really big game - our first European Cup visit to the continent. We had heard so much about the San Siro stadium and had expected a 90,000 all-seater stadium, but it was just a sea of concrete steps. Before the kick-off, some players like to spend a few minutes in the toilet contemplating the next 90 minutes. Well in keeping with the stadium design, the dressing room facilities in Milan were little more than holes in the floor. It was a bit embarrassing for the seasoned professionals wanting to fulfil their pre-match routine or for those desiring a private function. You feel inhibited with your mates glancing over at you. It was tough for everyone, but I have a lasting memory of an 18-year old debutante doing what became known as 'The San Siro Squat'.

Everton Career

	appearances				goals			
	League	FA Cup	FL Cup	Europe	League	FA Cup	FL Cup	Europe
1966/67	41	6	0	4	15	2	0	1
1967/68	34	4	2	0	20	0	0	0
1968/69	40	5	4	0	16	0	2	0
1969/70	37	1	3	0	10	1	1	0
1970/71	39	5	1	6	2	2	0	3
1971/72	17	0	0	0	3	0	0	0
Total	**208**	**21**	**10**	**10**	**66**	**5**	**3**	**4**

Alan Ball

observations of his team-mates

ALAN JAMES BALL

He was the World Cup
hero who re-defined
the requirements of
the modern midfielder.

Ball had flamboyant skills,
indefatigable stamina
and an astonishing
will to win.

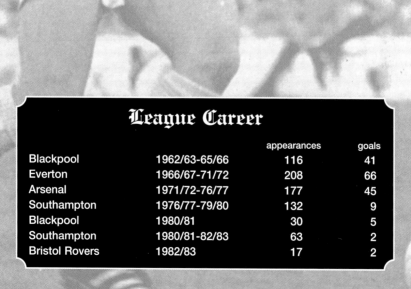

League Career

		appearances	goals
Blackpool	1962/63-65/66	116	41
Everton	1966/67-71/72	208	66
Arsenal	1971/72-76/77	177	45
Southampton	1976/77-79/80	132	9
Blackpool	1980/81	30	5
Southampton	1980/81-82/83	63	2
Bristol Rovers	1982/83	17	2

God sent you from heaven ...

As a schoolboy I was rejected by Wolves, but I'd set my heart on being a professional footballer and was eventually taken on as an amateur by Bolton. Unfortunately my fiery temperament got me into trouble and, shortly after my sixteenth birthday, the Burnden Park management advised my father: "*Alan is too small. He'd be better off trying to become a jockey.*" Subsequently Ronnie Suart offered me an apprenticeship at Blackpool and my career took off. After making my debut for the Tangerines at Anfield, with a victory over Liverpool in the first game back in the top flight, I made rapid progress at Bloomfield Road and soon collected my share of honours - Under-23 and full-international caps - and ultimately helped England capture the Jules Rimet trophy. But I also realised that I needed a bigger stage.

The papers reported that several clubs were interested but Don Revie was determined to take me to Elland Road. He had told me: "*With Bremner, Giles and Ball in the same side, we'll be unbeatable.*" He also encouraged me to dig my heels in for a transfer and compensated me with under-the-counter-payments. I got fined for revealing that in my autobiography '*All About A Ball*' but I'm sure that I wasn't the only player who had been paid in that way. Eventually Harry Catterick got me and I believe that Revie cried on the night that I joined Everton. I'm not sure if that was because he hadn't signed me or if he was regretting paying £300 for nothing. I'll never know if I'd have fitted in with Revie's ideas at club level, because I certainly didn't at international level.

Harry Catterick didn't have to sell Everton to me, they were my kind of club, but the thing that swung it for me was that Goodison was just down the East Lancs Road. Although I was a World Cup winner, I was still only a boy. I'd been brought up to respect great players and I was surrounded by some truly great ones at Everton. I knew that the royal blue fans were knowledgeable and that if I gave them value for money they'd take me to their hearts. I scored the only goal on my debut at Craven Cottage and, as I strolled along the Euston platform afterwards, a fan rushed up to me and threw himself onto his knees: "*Alan Ball, God sent you from heaven to Everton just to score goals like that.*" I also made a smashing start at Goodison seven days later against the Reds. I revelled in the atmosphere and grabbed two goals in the first 20 minutes. As a result, Gwladys Street started singing my name - I'd never experienced anything like it. That is not until the FA Cup clash with Liverpool in 1967 when there was over 65,000 packed into Goodison and another 40,000 glued to the giant screens at Anfield. I got the winner on the stroke of half-time, I've never hit a volley as sweetly in my life and recall thinking that this was the stage for me. I enjoyed a wonderful relationship with the royal blue fans and remember walking to the ground one day with bags in each hand. As a fan approached me with his autograph book in hand, I apologised: "*I'm sorry but I've got my hands full.*" He answered: "*That's okay Alan, just spit in my book!*"

My game changed towards the latter part of my Goodison days. I couldn't get up and down the pitch as often as I would've liked but nevertheless retained my never-say-die approach to the game - something I'd inherited from my dad. He taught me never to pull the wool over anyone's eyes, always give to 100%, to stain my shirt with blood, sweat and tears and play my natural game. I wasn't the nicest person on the pitch, but my dad used to say: "*The more they hate you, the better footballer you will be.*" That's the way it was, even with my team-mates.

Alan Ball

Alan Ball

Manchester United   August 31, 1966

Signed from Blackpool just before the start of the season. Born Farnworth and as a youngster was also a useful boxer. Contemplated a boxing career, but in 1961 became an apprentice at Blackpool. Made his England debut three days before his 20th birthday in 1965/66 and starred in the World Cup.

Arsenal   April 25, 1967

One of England's and Everton's most valuable assets, he cost a British record fee when transferred from Blackpool last August. He was a key member of England's victorious World Cup squad, and against Scotland 10 days ago he won his 18th full cap. He has also been capped at Under-23 level eight times. Ball started with Blackpool, signing professional forms in August 1962. A scorer as well as a schemer, he has one of the highest work-rates among modern players. Born Farnworth.

Nottingham Forest   April 22, 1968

Like Ray Wilson was a member of the England World Cup-winning team and joined Everton in exchange for over £100,000 and, as he's only 22, must surely turn out to be a bargain even at this price! He's a maker of opportunities and an excellent footballer with bags of determination but with two other priceless assets for he can play in most forward positions with equal skill and can score goals with consummate ease! He will not be on duty tonight due to his two-week suspension, which commenced last Monday.

Sheffield Wednesday   April 4, 1970

One of the outstanding personalities of the decade. Already an established England player when signed from Blackpool for a six-figure fee in 1966. He made his international debut as a teenager in 1965 and looks certain to appear in his second World Cup competition in Mexico later this year. Made a goal-scoring debut for Everton at Fulham on August 20, 1966 and has now scored well over 50 goals for the club.

Arsenal   October 17, 1970

Took over from Brian Labone as Everton's captain this season, and his football is even more colourful than his red hair and white boots. Was already firmly established in the England side when transferred from Blackpool for £100,000 in August 1966. Perpetual-motion player who includes two World Cup tournaments among his 45 England caps. 5 ft 7 in, 10 st.

Crystal Palace   May 1, 1971

A star of two World Cups, Alan's cap total is around the half-century mark. As a boy Alan was turned away by Bolton Wanderers. With tears of anger in his eyes he told his dad, now manager at Preston, "You see, I'll play for England when I'm 20." And he kept his promise! Alan demanded a trial at Blackpool. They signed him on the spot. Shortly after the 1966 World Cup, he moved to Everton for a £112,000 fee. Alan was a disappointed member of Everton's 1968 Wembley team.

Nottingham Forest   December 11, 1971

Like many of his England colleagues, Alan suffered the anticipated after-effects of the Mexico World Cup games last season and for the first time failed to register double figures in his goals record. Following a run with the Under-23's he won the first of his 50 full caps before his 21st birthday. No one who saw it will forget Alan's greatest match in the 1966 World Cup final. Soon after he moved to Everton for a £112,000 fee. Has completed his second century of games for the Blues.

Programme Pen Pictures

Impressions of Alan Ball ...

Alan Ball was one of the proudest players ever to have pulled on the shirts of Everton and England.

Howard Kendall: I first ran into that famous mop of red hair when he was playing for Blackpool against Preston. In those early days he was a non-stop player who was very difficult to mark and it was no surprise to me that he developed into one of the greatest players of all time. Some years ago I wrote in my book '*Nothing But The Best Is Good Enough*' that Alan Ball and Trevor Francis were the players who had impressed me the most - that's how highly I rated him. Colin and I were very fortunate to have someone like him to make up our midfield trio.

Alex Young: Several top clubs had been vying for his signature and in some small way I may have helped him make up his mind. Apparently when Harry Catterick was romancing him, Bally had watched us thrash Wednesday 5-1. I'd had a glory night and he told the manager that he'd join Everton only if he played alongside me. And for a while I started wide right to him. To be honest he never looked exceptional in training, but was inspirational on matchdays with his marvellous touch and insatiable appetite for work. He would run for 90 minutes and when the chips were down, he would run even harder. Bally would strut around the park with swaggering self-belief, but if we'd fallen behind at half-time, he'd tear his hair out with frustration and would sometimes cry with anger in defeat. He was a superb motivator but definitely not a diplomat. I roomed with him and know that he wasn't shy to criticise team-mates. He thought that if he was getting kicked upside down then it was the job of Labby and our defenders to reciprocate and clatter their forwards every now and then. Because he was half-a-dozen years younger than me, he liked to ask my advice about things and, of course, sought guidance from his father. Bally adored his dad who was never short of advice for his superstar son. He'd joke: "*If you are playing badly - get yourself sent off. Just get your name in the Sunday papers.*"

Colin Harvey: The Monday after we'd been turned over by Liverpool in the Charity Shield, the boss completed his shrewdest deal of all time by signing Alan Ball. Twelve days later, we murdered the red champions 3-1. That result announced to Merseyside and to the football world that Bally had arrived. He was the greatest that I ever played alongside, a brilliant passer and a sharp thinker whose enthusiasm made me push myself that little bit harder. Alan was the catalyst for a glorious four-year spell of rich and flowing football.

Roger Kenyon: Bally's strength of character made those around him feel at least 10 feet tall. He demanded impeccably high standards from everybody, irrespective of his own form. That led to one or two confrontations with team-mates on the pitch as well as in the dressing room. But he never tangled with me, he liked to call me 'The Assassin'.

Keith Newton: Alan was a fabulous player for Everton and for England, but by the time that he had left the club he'd driven us all mad with his incessant moaning. I think that he was frustrated by his inability to reproduce the form to which he'd become so accustomed. I vividly remember one incident at Elland Road when Alan raced back to have a go at the defence after we'd conceded a sloppy goal. We felt that his whinging was uncalled for and that he'd be better occupied getting up the pitch and doing his own job. So when he left the club it shouldn't have been a shock to any of us. It was almost a relief.

Tommy Wright: If things weren't going too well during a match, Alan would always have something to say. No-one was spared from his brutal honesty and his relentless shouting, but that was the way he played the game.

Ray Wilson: World-class players rarely string together more than three or four outstanding performances, but Alan Ball could play 12 blinders on the trot.

Born: Farnworth - May 12, 1945
Everton registration date: August 15, 1966
Everton debut: Fulham at Craven Cottage on August 20, 1966
Final Everton appearance: Derby County at Baseball Ground on December 18, 1971

Tommy Jackson: Alan Ball was an ordinary man with extra-ordinary abilities. He was a true superstar even though we treated him like one of the lads. I'd been a part-timer with Glentoran before joining Everton in 1967 and was overwhelmed by the immense abilities of someone who had already won the World Cup but was only my age. He was a committed competitor whether in training or on the international stage and I recall that we enjoyed some particularly tough exchanges in the Northern Ireland-England match in 1969. He was handicapped by a nose injury that day and we didn't exchange shirts after the game. I wasn't too bothered because his was stained with blood - his own.

John Hurst: Bally's enthusiasm got him into trouble with referees, but he was so talented that he rarely got into trouble with the ball. He was the best one-touch player that I've ever seen. You could hit a ball up to him and before it had arrived he knew what he was doing with it.

Gordon West: Bally probably cleaned my boots at Blackpool, but had matured into a fabulous player by the time he'd arrived at Goodison. I've never come across anyone who hated to lose as much as he did and can vividly remember the scenes after an unexpected set-back. Our new captain was in tears saying: *"What will my dad say when I get home, he'll kill me."* I'm honoured to have played in his team and I'd pick him for my own team any day of the week, but I'm not sure that I'd go out for a drink with him - no doubt he'd say the same about me.

Brian Labone: Alan Ball was a national hero having already had a World Cup winner's medal, but we teased him that if he'd have showed up only a few months earlier he may have had an FA Cup winner's medal to go with it. After all Ray Wilson had got both. I'd already met him at England get-togethers and knew that he was far too good for Blackpool. He'd played against us in the infamous fixture when 16-year old Joe Royle had made his debut and some hooligans had supposedly jostled Harry Catterick. Blackpool won 2-0 and Bally took the piss by sitting on the ball. At Goodison he was an immediate success - white boots and all. Of course, he could be a real ball of fire but then he wouldn't have been the player that he was without his combustible temperament. He combined boundless energy with great skills and would try to play every position on the pitch, except centre-half because he couldn't head the ball. He was also a formidable competitor, a battler, a winner - some times a whiner - and you would often see him going around pointing fingers at opponents and stirring up trouble.

David Johnson: He'd berate himself mercilessly throughout the game in order to bring out the best in his game and tried to goad everybody else in the same way - it wasn't well received.

Sandy Brown: He was a tremendous player - one of the all-time greats of the game - but was far too mouthy for my liking. He knew how to wind people up and sometimes referred to Labby as 'Mr Softy' behind his back, whereas Labby would call him 'Bawly' to his face. Tommy Wright and Labby must have got used to him telling them how to defend because they both played with him in the England team. When I think of it, Bally could have yapped for his country.

Howard Kendall: Alan could be unkind to his team-mates. I remember one day at Bellefield, he had his arms stretched out appealing: *"How can I play with this lot?"* We laughed because only a few months earlier we'd won the championship, but perhaps it was a sign of things to come. If we were losing he'd vent his frustrations by sprinting 20 yards to kick someone up in the air and blame the rest of us for getting him booked. It was his way of demonstrating to everyone the will to win that burned inside him. We understood that it was a part of him but it wasn't a part that we liked. Alan was appointed captain in 1970 in an attempt to temper his effervescent behaviour but it wasn't one of the manager's finer decisions. He'd often disappear up to Catterick's office and during our next training session Wilf Dixon would bring to our attention: *"Alan is not getting the ball the right way"* or *"Alan is not getting the right service."*

Blue Blooded Aristocrats

interviews with their team-mates

Los Tres Magníficos ...

Kendall, Harvey & Ball were the greatest midfield union ever fielded by a British club and were the driving force behind a team respected for their entertaining football.

Gordon West: Kendall, Harvey & Ball was the best midfield trio that I've ever known. I used to stand back and marvel at the way they played. 'The Toffee Triangle' was so dominant, I'd little else to do! They were the heartbeat of the best side I ever played in and won the 69/70 title race at a canter. We were actually crowned champions on the first day of April, with several games in hand, and took great pride in the fact that we captured the championship by playing the game in the cultured tradition of the Goodison School of Science.

Howard Kendall: We played some beautiful football - the best that I have been associated with - and consequently our midfield unit received perhaps more than its fair share of publicity. Labby liked to remind everyone at Bellefield that we were more than a three-man team. He also loved to give us labels and one of his favourites was 'Los Tres Magnificos'. Labby and Westie would joke that we were the only three-man team to have won the League championship!

Brian Labone: When you're a member of a winning side, you don't mind that the praise is heaped on three very highly skilled aristocrats. Of course, our squad contained numerous internationals and just as many unsung heroes who contributed to the success of the team. Possibly Colin, with his incredible close-ball control, was the most skilful of the magnificent midfield trio. Quite definitely Bally was the hardest grafter that I've ever come across and Howard was a superb ball-winner who had made tackling into an art form. Our No 4 could also crack them in from outside of the box and our No 8 could knock them in from the six-yard line, 20 times a season, but our No 6 would save his strikes for the big occasions.

Alex Young: In some ways they were like chalk and cheese, but when dressed in royal blue they shared many of the same qualities - impeccable ball control. powerful engines, immense courage, infectious enthusiasm and the desire to battle for one another. Understandably we sought to capitalise on their extra-ordinary footballing abilities and would constantly play through midfield - much to the delight of the Goodison congregation.

Ray Wilson: By 1968, I'd realised that the manager had assembled a team of true quality. Playing alongside Kendall, Harvey & Ball was so easy - all I had to do was get the ball to them and they would do the rest. My only regret was that I was 10 years older than them.

John Hurst: Three-man midfields had usually consisted of a passer, a runner and a hard-case. But 'The Holy Trinity' was different. All three had great vision, incredible stamina and were tremendous at playing one-twos.

Colin Harvey: Harvey, Kendall & Ball were just the icing on a very tasty Goodison cake. I believe that we played our best football towards the middle of the 68/69 season, however, we were tougher in the championship campaign and won away games that we'd previously have drawn. It may sound immodest but we knew that we were capable of beating everyone. The famous banner wasn't unfurled until after I'd departed for Sheffield Wednesday in September 1974. I didn't see it myself because I was playing for my new club at Bolton, but my mates had gone to watch Everton versus Wolves and told me all about a huge white sheet that had been draped over the criss-crosses of the old Park End stand christening me 'The White Pele'. It gave me a great sense of pride to think that I was being remembered in that way by the fans that I had grown up with as well as a sense of humility to be compared with the greatest footballer of all time.

Joe Royle: Kendall, Harvey & Ball were famed for their sublime ball skills and slick passing. They choreographed some sensational team displays, but their true greatness was reflected in their ability to turn in consistent and whole-hearted performances week in and week out. The stars of the midfield may have been the darlings of the Goodison faithful but they always considered themselves to be just one part of a very good Everton team.

Alan Ball: We not only wanted to be great for each other but also to be better than each other. Colin, Howard and I developed a special understanding and could've found one another in the dark. We'd blitz teams at home and away and won the Division 1 title with a haul of 66 points, that was in the days of two points for a win, and finished nine points ahead of Leeds United, the runners-up, and 15 points ahead of Liverpool. We were far and away the best side in the land and for me to captain Everton during the 69/70 run-in was an extra-special honour. We were more than worthy champions. On today's basis it was like winning the championship by 17 points, which was an incredible margin considering the number of good teams in the League in those days.

Tommy Wright: We'd matured into a very good side by the second-half of the 68/69 season and were in a class of our own throughout the following campaign. Given our improved consistency, we were confident that we'd win the title and it was always a case of who would be the bridesmaid. The side was well-balanced and had few weaknesses. Under the guidance of Brian Labone, we had the best defence in the League and with Joe Royle, Jimmy Husband and Alan Whittle up-front, we had a potent young strike-force with an average age of 20. And of course, we also had Howard Kendall, Colin Harvey and Alan Ball who could play a bit in midfield. Harry Catterick's approach to every game was simple. He instructed us to get the ball and to give it to 'The Holy Trinity' - and they would do the rest. It was a joy to be in a team that oozed confidence and played such beautiful football. Some of the stuff that we played at home was truly magnificent and every team was scared stiff to come to Goodison Park. The fans loved it but for some reason we never got the credit nation-wide for the quality of the football that we served up.

Jimmy Husband: Our kits were set out in numerical order and I had the privilege of changing between Colin and Bally. For two guardians of the beautiful game, they weren't a pretty sight on the rare occasions when we lost. Because they didn't take defeat well, I'd get changed and hop onto the team bus as quickly as possible. But it was great to be a part of something so very special. We were encouraged to play fast, flowing football with lots of running off the ball and lots of interchanging short passes and our efforts were rewarded with a rich harvest of goals. Even though we were near-invincible throughout the 69/70 season, I believe that we played our best football during the previous campaign. We had some tremendous one-touch players in our ranks and when the midfield trio was injury-free, they managed to bring out the best in all of us. It was hardly surprising that opponents seemed to wilt at the prospect of being out-classed by them. I remember that we kicked off the championship campaign with convincing triumphs over Arsenal at Highbury and Manchester United at Old Trafford but reserved our best performances for Goodison where we hammered the other leading contenders - Leeds 3-2 and Chelsea 5-2. Unfortunately, I had to sit out the last few months through injury and it was only when I was restricted to the sidelines that I realised just how dominant we had become.

David Johnson: Howard, Colin and Bally played some truly magnificent football, much of it off the cuff. When I was breaking through into the first-team, the boss preferred to play with two wingers in front of them and with Big Joe as centre-forward. I was slighter and quicker but it was only after I'd moved on to Ipswich Town that my more mobile style of play became fashionable. I would've loved to have been around a season or two earlier.

Alan Whittle: The 69/70 run-in was a fairy-tale experience for me. Kendall, Harvey & Ball simply beat opponents into submission at Goodison where white flags were a basic feature of the visitor's dug-out. As a 19-year old novice, I felt privileged to be involved in the action and relished the challenge of applying the finishing touches. I grabbed 11 goals in 15 outings.

Roger Kenyon: I watched most of the games in the championship season from the bench. It was like having a season-ticket to the best seat at Goodison. We were solid in defence, potent in attack and simply dominated opponents in midfield to capture the title. I like to think that I played my part in deputising for Brian Labone in the last eight games of the season, of which we won seven and drew the other, but I regret that the greatest skipper in the history of the club didn't get the recognition he deserved at the final-whistle of the West Brom game.

Johnny Morrissey: Harry Catterick discovered the perfect midfield blend. Howard was the best ball-winner in the game at the time, Colin was the little ratter with lots of stamina and pace and Bally was the key link between defence and attack. The rest of us simply played to our strengths. Jimmy Husband, who was really mobile, would make diagonal runs to support Joe Royle up front and Bally had so much energy that he could also get into the final-third to support them. If we were under pressure, I'd serve as the get-out man. I had the strength and nous to hold the ball up and would convert into a fourth midfielder. Most Division 1 sides had a dedicated ball-winner in midfield but 'The Holy Trinity' did the same job with finesse rather than fury. Of course neither Kendall nor Harvey was reluctant to put his foot in, but the Everton midfield generally won possession by thinking quicker than opponents, anticipating play, and chasing balls that everyone else had given up for dead. Their courage took them into hostile situations where the studs were flying but more often than not one of them would emerge in control of the ball and ready to make a decisive pass. Bally was also a great improviser and, if things weren't going our way, he would have a word in my ear and we'd concentrate on playing neat one-twos in order to get some rhythm into the team's play.

Terry Darracott: Kendall, Harvey & Ball were the top three players in the country and were synonymous with cultured football. They had different personalities but were good mates off the pitch. I only played a bit part at the time, getting in the first-team now and again, but not a day went by when I didn't thank my lucky stars that I was training with them.

Sandy Brown: 'The Holy Trinity' overwhelmed opponents and I think that we only lost 10 or so games during two full seasons. Sadly one of those defeats is etched on my soul as well as my memory. Every day for the past 30 years I have been reminded that our worst League result during that run was the home defeat to Liverpool in early-December 1969. It was a derby game that I'll never be allowed to forget because I scored the most spectacular own goal in the history of Merseyside football. I can still see the cross hitting John Hurst on the shoulder and dropping invitingly into the penalty area. I was aware that I would have to use the top of my head to lift it over the bar for a corner, but I caught it with my forehead and finished on my hands and knees facing the cheering red hordes on the Park End terraces. Westie growled: *"Good goal Sandy!"* I replied: *"It was a fucking back-pass, where were you?"* I can't remember what Bally shouted at me but I can still feel his eyes piercing my back to this day.

George Telfer: I was thrilled to sign apprentice forms in 1970 and was immediately in awe of the magnificent skills of Kendall, Harvey & Ball. I'd never seen anything like them. Despite their god-like status, they trained hard every day and were full of encouragement for the lads on the fringes of the first-team. It was a turbulent period at Bellefield with Bally signing for Arsenal, Colin leaving for Sheffield, before returning to supervise the youth development programme, and Howard eventually moving on to Birmingham, but I feel really honoured to have had the opportunity of wearing the blue and white of Everton alongside them.

Bellefield boot-camp ...

Harry Catterick assembled 'The Holy Trinity'. The Everton manager was renowned for being a stern disciplinarian and players crossed him at their peril.

Gordon Watson: The manager would punish players for arriving late. Irrespective of their status, Alan Ball and the rest of the lads had to sign the book kept near the entrance at Bellefield. At precisely 10 o'clock a red line was inserted and all late-comers had to sign below it. Despite this strict regime, or because of it, they were a lovely bunch of lads. We never told them how to play. We simply concentrated on honing their ball skills and physical fitness. That sounds a bit primitive but it was a giant step from my playing days at Everton, when we only got a ball out on Tuesdays.

Alan Whittle: I made my debut at The Hawthorns shortly after my eighteenth birthday - in that glorious 6-2 hammering when Bally scored four times. But it could have been much earlier. The previous season I'd been invited to travel with the first-team to Wolverhampton but mis-timed my arrival at Bellefield. In other words I missed the team coach. I'm sure that the manager would have waited for any of the established stars but he refused to wait four minutes for an apprentice who was about to make his debut. The only person hanging around the training ground was Howard Kendall who had been sidelined by injury for a couple weeks. Although he had not planned to travel to the match, Howard came to my rescue and drove me to the Midlands in his new Jag. We arrived at Molineux before the team coach and as I waited in the visitors' dressing room I worried about how I would explain my tardiness to the boss. Well, I shouldn't have bothered because he ignored me and obviously didn't pick me to play. But he did say a few words to me before the kick-off: *"Come and see me on Monday morning."* He fined me £5 - which was about a week's wages. Later on in my professional career I learned to follow the advise of the legendary American grid-iron coach, Vince Lombardi of the Green Bay Packers, and set my watch five minutes fast.

Howard Kendall: Harry Catterick was fully aware that he intimidated his players. He liked to spy on us from his Bellefield office and we learned to monitor any movement of his blinds of his office window. He only graced the training field if a club director or the television cameras made a visit and would appear in his new tracksuit and plimsolls. The boss was very fortunate because every player in the country wanted to wear blue and white in those days and he had the funds at his beck and call to buy the very best. He could target the players that he wanted as soon as they became available. However, I believe that over time the changing workings of the transfer market lessened his effectiveness. There wasn't a great deal of coaching at Bellefield. Catterick valued balance - it was one reason why we gelled so quickly. We were a balanced midfield unit in a balanced team. All three of us were well aware that we had world-class defenders behind us and super strikers up front. Usually we adopted a 4-3-3 formation, which could be intuitively changed to 4-4-2. Johnny Morrissey hugged the left touchline, perhaps more so than on the right where Jimmy Husband was a floater. Jimmy would join Joe Royle at the front and leave a hole that I had to cover. We played some great football, most of it off the cuff, and never worried about the opposition. I remember during one game, the full-back followed Jimmy away from the flank and left a big open space. When the ball was played from Johnny to Colin, I moved round into this space and Colin instinctively hit the switch ball to the right-hand side for me to feed Big Joe. Well the following Monday, Wilf Dixon decided to put on a coaching session and used the Bellefield blackboard to propose the exact move that we had improvised. Bally was unimpressed and barked *"We did that on Saturday!"* His feedback wasn't well received by Catterick's right-hand man. Despite our tactical naiveté, we possessed the advantage of having players who could read the game. Some days at Goodison it was no contest - a battle of wits against unarmed opponents!

Brian Labone: You knew where you were with the boss. Sometimes he catered to Bally a bit more than anyone else but that was understandable because he was the biggest attraction at Goodison since 'The Golden Vision'. We certainly weren't over-coached but now and then Wilf Dixon would chalk out a game plan. The only problem was that the blackboard foes were static, whereas our opponents moved around on the pitch. Understandably, we preferred to rely on the astute football brains of Kendall, Harvey & Ball. The midfield adopted a fiddler's elbow formation and could be 30 yards apart. Of course, they weren't cursed with too many loose passes from defence and didn't have to spend too much time scrapping for possession.

Keith Newton: There was far too much emphasis on physical fitness at Bellefield. The training regime was very hard and, as a consequence, some of the older players would pick up strains. But Wilf Dixon wouldn't listen to our complaints.

Tommy Wright: Modern footballers are athletes. In my day we had a basic routine - warm up, ball work, stamina training and 5-a-side to finish off. It was the same every day except Fridays when we'd have a team-talk and work out tactics for the game. Harry Catterick went about his business quietly but knew exactly what he wanted.

Alan Ball: We were the fittest team I've ever come across in the game and we were motivated by fear. 'The Catt' frightened me. His disciplinarian-style could maintain a strong hold over most players for three years maximum but after that he didn't seem such a formidable figure and the players no longer responded. I've thought long and hard about why we failed to build on our success. I've likened it to training a puppy - you smack it when it's young to teach it to do the things you want, but in the end it bites back because it has wised up.

Colin Harvey: Catterick was a top manager for 14 years and his record compares with those of Revie, Busby, Nicholson and Shankly. I'm disappointed that he has never got the credit he deserved. He created two championship-winning sides and finished outside the top six only once - and that was in 1966 when we won the FA Cup. I found that if you worked hard then you had no problems with him. He wasn't a master tactician - he just let us get on with it. Very often he'd pit the forwards against the defenders and this led to something of an altercation between Tommy Wright and Johnny Morrissey. Tommy was like greased lightning and had intercepted all the passes intended for Johnny, much to the annoyance of the winger. After a while Johnny resorted to threats: *"Let some of these balls go through to me or I'll do you."* Tommy ignored him and eventually training had to be abandoned as our legendary winger chased our England fullback around Bellefield. I really looked forward to training. I loved it so much that I set up a circuit in my mother's garage and did that three afternoons a week using a tennis ball. It helped to improve my touch.

Terry Darracott: A top player is just a talented player who's prepared to work extra hard. Bally would return to the gym and do sprints and Colin and Howard would also come back in the afternoon and join in with the kids. They were great role models and would always pass on advice. Some players don't have the mental and physical attributes required to mix it with the best - Kendall, Harvey & Ball did. They were top players with no obvious weaknesses.

Jimmy Husband: Towards the end of my career I played for Memphis Rouges. During their close-season I would come back to Merseyside and keep fit by doing a spot of running. If I had a bit of a strain I would drop in at Bellefield for treatment. One morning I noticed an old guy lying on his belly on one of the physio's beds. As I settled on the other bed I heard an unmistakable voice: *"How you doing son? How's the family? How's it going in America?"* It was Shanks. I think that it was the most interest that any manager had shown in my welfare at Bellefield for quite some time!

Jimmy Gabriel: Harry was the figure at the window watching us train. He was pretty strict but fair, and liked to keep us on our toes.

Gordon West: The likes of Bally and Colin were svelte human pipe-cleaners whereas Big Joe, Darce and I would struggle to meet our prescribed weights. My problem was simple - if we'd had a good result, I'd put on seven pounds celebrating over the weekend. We were weighed at Bellefield every Friday morning by Arthur Proudler, one of our trainers. I was terrified of being found over-weight and would starve myself on Thursdays in a vain effort to reach my target of 14 stones 7 pounds. I'd get on the scales and shout: *"Arthur, I'm spot on 14-2."* Of course he wasn't aware that I was holding on to the edge of his table. This went on for weeks until Wilf Dixon rumbled me. He grabbed my arm and all of a sudden I'd gained 10 pounds.

Tommy Jackson: 'The Catt' was a tyrannical taskmaster. We trained hard at Bellefield and most of us had to skip breakfast in order to stay within our weight limits. I remember that we'd be running circuits and building up our stamina, but all we could smell was his breakfast being cooked in the canteen. There's nothing quite like the smell of fried bacon and sausage and to have it wafting all round the training ground when we were all ravenous was bordering on cruel.

Roger Kenyon: The boss ruled with a rod of iron and could be difficult to get along with. I'd come through the ranks and knew no difference, but some of the senior players found him hard to take. I always thought that he was someone who knew what he was doing. Our tactics involved lots of improvisation. Of course Labby as well as Bally, Howard and Colin provided lots of advice - namely to play the ball through midfield.

Alex Young: My life changed the day that Harry Catterick arrived. In many ways the club was less professional than Hearts and changes were needed, but the new manager installed a regime of fear. I never liked the man and have no doubt that I was on his black-list from the start. He suspected that I thought that he wasn't always looking after the best interests of Everton. Most of the time he ignored me. If we had played exceptionally well, he'd welcome us back into the dressing room: *"Well done! Howard! Great game, Alan! All right, Alex?"* I strongly believe that the only players he wanted to succeed were those he'd brought through the ranks and the ones he'd spent money on. His dealings produced Ball and Kendall but he was too quick to get rid of Collins, Vernon and, of course, Bally. All of them loved Everton.

Alan Whittle: I was a mere baby when Catterick called me: *"the greatest Everton discovery of all time."* I may have impressed the manager but I think that his coaching staff were a bit intimidated by my self-confidence. They must have thought that I could look after myself because they made few arrangements to protect me on the pitch. In contrast Wilf Dixon and Bally seemed to have a good relationship at Blackpool - at Everton - at Arsenal

Frank D'arcy: We all had to sign-in by 10 am and Gordon Watson would write the time next to your name so that Harry Catterick could see who was late. I lived in Tancred Road, only about 30 minutes from Bellefield, but was always late. I'd a list of excuses but none of them impressed the boss and my punishment was an afternoon of training. Although I was really fit, I struggled to stay at my target weight of 11-3. Therefore, along with Westie, I had to endure extra training to keep it under control. In one particular session we had to sprint the length of one touch-line and back along the other within 45 seconds while wearing two shirts, two pairs of shorts and two pairs of socks under my heavy tracksuit. I then had to jog back to the start and repeat the exercise five more times under the watchful eyes of Messrs Dixon, Borrowdale, Proudler and Catterick. I was near-exhaustion but confident that I'd lost the required six pounds. However when I enquired as to the whereabouts of our bulky keeper, the boss rubbed his hands together in his characteristic manner and declared: *"The big fella is at the dentist."*

The unsung cast ...

Kendall, Harvey & Ball enjoyed the limelight but the Everton squad embraced many players who never got the credit that their contributions deserved. They included Morrissey, Jackson, Brown, Whittle, Kenyon ...

John Hurst: Johnny Morrissey was one of the toughest players I've ever seen. He was always first pick in 5-a-sides because nobody in their right mind wanted to be kicked by him.

Brian Labone: Bobby Collins and Tony Kay possessed something that the members of 'The Holy Trinity' didn't - they were hard. If it hadn't been for Mike Gabbert of *The People* and the infamous soccer bribes scandal, I've few doubts that Tony Kay, the only arrogant bastard in the 62/63 team, would have made the 1966 World Cup squad and the Everton midfield would have evolved into Kendall, Harvey, Ball and Kay. Of course 'The Holy Trinity' had a truly tough guy at their sides - Johnny Morrissey. Forget about 'Anfield Iron' Smith, 'Chopper' Harris, 'Bite Your Legs' Hunter and their macho reputations, many full-backs can testify that Johnny could be brutal. A product of the Scottie Road School of Science, no-one wanted to play against him - not even in training. Johnny was also a quality winger who needed his muscle-man's physique to carry his tons of genuine skill. Another unsung Blue who could look after himself was Tommy Jackson. I recall that the Northern Ireland star did a magnificent job in the 1968 semi-final when Bally was suspended. Tommy was an Irish terrier who made major contributions when Howard or Colin were injured or when Bally was otherwise unavailable. I don't know why the two of them never got along but they would go after one another in training - they didn't need a ball. Bally could be very critical of less gifted players. One of his taunts was: *"That fellow can trap a ball farther than I can kick it!"*

Alex Young: If Tony Kay hadn't got himself into trouble, I don't think there would have been a 'Holy Trinity' phenomenon. He was a show-man, a truly great footballer and a tragic loss to Everton and to England. During my career, I'd say that Dave MacKay was the best player at Hearts and Alan Ball was the maestro at Goodison, but pushing them both was Tony. He liked to clatter opponents - Bally would've loved him. Some people claimed that he would have kicked his own mother if she'd dwelled on the ball. I'd say that he was nastier than Kendall, Harvey & Ball put together. Johnny Morrissey was another hard man. Everyone tip-toed around him, even Tony. Johnny picked up a championship medal in 1963 but really didn't blossom until his last three seasons at Goodison when there wasn't a better winger in the game. He combined well with the midfield trio and they relied upon him as an important fourth partner. Another players' player was Tommy Jackson. If any of the midfield aces were absent, he would try to fill their shoes. He was a good little battler - brave and full of running.

Tommy Jackson: I arrived on the Saturday and, with Alan Ball suspended, was thrown straight into a Tuesday night game at Forest and by the end of my first week was playing against Leeds United in the FA Cup semi-final. My baptism was made a lot easier by Labby who settled me down and by Johnny Morrissey who got the winner from the spot. Over the next few seasons I was lucky enough to come into the team when either Colin, Howard or Alan couldn't play, for one reason or another. It didn't take long to get to know them and the way that they played. During the championship season I deputised for Colin seven times, Howard six times and even Bally on one occasion and like to think, in my own small way, that I contributed to the Kendall, Harvey & Ball legend. But unlike my team-mates I only got to play in the same team as all three members of 'The Holy Trinity' on two occasions.

Johnny Morrissey: I didn't mind being the unsung hero of Harry's team. I was picked for the Football League in 1969 but unfortunately Sir Alf Ramsey thought that I was too much of an out-and-out winger for his preferred formation.

Howard Kendall: Football was a squad game even back in the 1960s and Tommy Jackson was an unsung hero. If one of us was injured or if Bally had had a run-in with a referee, then Tommy could be relied upon to do a good job for us. He certainly earned his League championship medal.

Colin Harvey: Before the arrival of Alan Ball and Howard Kendall, Harry Catterick had been building his team around Tony Kay. He was a magnificent player who possessed the qualities that the boss admired - skill on the ball, strength in the tackle, and a tremendous will to win. Tony also had a mean streak. I vividly remember one incident at Bellefield. I must have been enjoying a particularly good time in midfield because the next minute I got a set of Tony's studs in my chest. Our own hard-case in the late-sixties, Johnny Morrissey, was probably the most under-rated player in the country. He was always easy to find when things were tight and could convert us from a 4-3-3 formation into a 4-4-2 team. Johnny could hold things up, was an accurate crosser and was very strong in the tackle. So strong that he even made it into Jack Charlton's infamous little black book. His ability to look after himself is legendary but never over-shadowed his tremendous skills. From time-to-time one of the midfield trio would be missing and Tommy Jackson would come in. He was tidy on the ball and was very effective at harassing opponents into making errors. Tommy was a real bargain at £9,000 from Glentoran. On the other hand, Ernie Hunt was something of an expensive enigma. The boss signed him after he'd had a couple of good games for Wolves against us in the FA Cup but soon realised that he wasn't going to fit in.

Jimmy Husband: I got my big break because of Ernie Hunt. He was a big money signing who had the misfortune to arrive at Goodison when the boss was experimenting with the 4-3-3 formation. He lacked the necessary mobility and after he'd had a dozen or so outings I got the chance of an extended run and poor Ernie was on his way to Coventry.

Frank D'arcy: I played eight games, made nine substitute appearances and was one of the best paid spectators during my nine years at the club. I did come off the bench on five occasions during the championship season, even replacing Bally against Manchester United. Of course I'd have liked to have featured in more games alongside the famous midfield triangle and would've loved to have played in the final home game against West Brom. I remember the lap of honour around Goodison, the atmosphere that day was electric - a bit like the Hall of Fame Dinner at the Adelphi.

Roger Kenyon: Even though Tommy Jackson was the automatic replacement in midfield and Sandy Brown was capable of turning his hand to any task, the manager wasn't reluctant to blood the talented kids from the club's nursery. He had confidence in the likes of Whittle, Johnson, Darracott, Jones and Lyons and even asked me to turn out in midfield. I wasn't known for my silky skills but I was never reluctant to put my foot in for Everton.

Gordon West: Kendall, Harvey & Ball had just begun to buzz when we played at St James's Park in late-1967. In those days it wasn't uncommon for the nastier forwards to bad-mouth or spit at the keeper. So I learned to retaliate by throwing the ball out with a clenched fist and if they didn't get out of my way then it was their own fault. Well this day a fella called Burton happened to get onto the end of my fist and, shortly after he hit the deck, the referee directed me towards the showers. Sandy Brown, who would play anywhere for Everton, pulled on my green shirt and the first time that he touched the ball was to pick it out of the net from the penalty kick. I sulked most of the way home on the coach until Sandy tried to console me by informing me that I'd ruined the game for him. I simply glared at him: *"I don't know what you are going on about, it was 0-0 when I came off!"* I had expected Bally to have a go at me, not an unsung hero like Alexander Dewar Brown.

Midfield warriors ...

English football was rich in quality midfielders in the sixties and games were won or lost in the trenches. Nevertheless, Kendall, Harvey & Ball received scant recognition in London.

Howard Kendall: Bremner and Giles were tremendous competitors. During one game, Johnny Giles six-studded my chest while I was on the deck. It's the type of thing that you never forget and the following season I tackled him in the early minutes at Elland Road. I prided myself in not committing nasty fouls or going over the top but I was always committed and on this occasion went through to take the ball and Giles. The little Irishman picked himself up on the perimeter track and returned to the pitch nodding to certain members of the Leeds mob. At that moment I realised that there was a contract out on me. Alan Ball whispered: "*I know that you are good at one-touch but may I suggest you get it down to half a touch today.*" A few minutes later Norman Hunter bit my right leg.

Alex Young: On their day, the Elland Road duo could play at the same heights as Kendall, Harvey & Ball, but never better. Giles could be a wee bit ugly and knew how to go over the top. Bobby Collins must have taught him. Of course there were some really good midfielders around like Peters, Hudson, Crerand, Hollins and Bell. Many were strong and robust, others had immense skills. But no other midfield had the combined qualities of the Everton boys.

Brian Labone: By the 67/68 season, that is by the time that the Kendall, Harvey & Ball unit had matured, they were by far the most influential midfield in the land. Of course, we should have dominated the next decade but unfortunately the championship-winning team was disbanded. The quality of 'The Holy Trinity' is reflected in the very good opponents who were around at that time such as Billy Bremner and Giles at Leeds, John Hollins and Hudson at Chelsea, Ian Callaghan and Hughes at Liverpool, Dave MacKay and Gemmill at Derby, Nobby Stiles and Crerand at United and Alan Oakes and 'Nijinsky' farther down the road at City.

Colin Harvey: The game in the sixties wasn't pre-occupied with off-side tactics and midfield players had much more room. The household names of those days would have been great players today. Bremner and Giles consistently gave us our most challenging contests.

Sandy Brown: Johnny Giles and Billy Bremner were the worst I've ever seen at going over the top. I got sent off in the first few minutes of one battle against them and the referee eventually had to take everyone off to calm things down. It got nasty when I went to chest the ball and Giles studded me, my shirt was ripped and my chest was bleeding. Before I retaliated, I told him: "*You've been asking for this Johnny.*" Then I punched his nose round to the other side of his face. I received a two-week suspension for my troubles and, to rub salt into my wounds, I didn't get paid during my suspension but still had to go to training.

Alan Ball: George Best arrived on the scene at about the same time as me. He had everything - skill, pace and courage - and could play on the wing or in midfield. He earned world-wide fame as an entertainer and was by far the best opponent I've ever came up against. In contrast I also believe that Ian Callaghan and Alan Oakes were two of the under-rated midfield warriors of my era. There were many others like them who did most of the work but got little of the glory.

George Best: A few scouts came to watch me play for my school, but at 5 ft 4 in and 7 stone they all said I was too small. The same experience befell Alan Ball and no clubs were willing to take a chance on him either. He was one of the most accomplished professionals to have played the beautiful game and I've always looked up to him because he also proved that if you're good enough, you're big enough. Alan was a very special footballer.

Ian Callaghan: The Everton trio were formidable. Shanks encouraged us to forget about our opponents and concentrate on our own strengths. Of course that was easier said than done when faced with a daunting battle against arguably the finest midfield unit of my generation.

Tommy Smith: Kendall, Harvey & Ball played like they were one person. They knew exactly what each other was going to do and complemented each other so well that they went on to be one of the greatest midfields that the game has ever produced. I've never known why they didn't get the accolades they deserved. Howard didn't even get an international cap. Bally probably got more plaudits than the other two lads put together. He was very competitive and you soon realised that you were in a battle when you played against him. He was a fiery lad and it was hard to dampen him down and no matter which way you went he always seemed to be there. He'd really get on my nerves - especially with that voice of his!

Brian Hall: If you actually sat down and thought about playing against them - the best midfield trio I've ever seen without a shadow of doubt - you wouldn't actually go out onto the park, you'd be too terrified.

Nobby Stiles: United didn't look forward to going to Goodison Park in those days and very rarely got a result. Kendall, Harvey & Ball were an incredible combination, as formidable as our own Law, Charlton and Best. It wasn't a case of just looking after one, they blended so well together that you had to keep an eye on all three. Colin was the quiet one who was so good that I used to call him 'Mr Smooth' and Howard was another very creative player who brought great balance to the Everton midfield. Of course, Bally was everywhere, he was like a perpetual motion machine. I knew him well and roomed with him at Hendon Hall during the 1966 World Cup tournament. As a devout Catholic, I'd get up at 7 o'clock every morning to go to mass in Golder's Green. The night before the final, I couldn't decide whether I should lie in and get a good rest or do the right thing. I decided to go to church, it was about quarter to seven and I sneaked out so as not to wake Alan up. It was only a couple of months ago when the World Cup lads were all together that he complained: *"You toothless bastard, you woke me up every single morning for three weeks!"* but it must have done him good because he was the best player on the pitch that day.

Duncan McKenzie: I had the misfortune to play against them for Nottingham Forest and got absolutely battered at Goodison. The main reason we were beaten so badly was that the Everton engine room was so dominant. They were famous throughout the land. You can go anywhere in the country and everybody knows of Kendall, Harvey & Ball.

Tommy Jackson: Ironically I played against Everton on my debut for Forest. Howard and Bally were partnered by Henry Newton that day and my old club lost 0-1. Bally seemed a little off colour and may have been carrying an injury because he didn't cover the same amount of ground as usual. It proved to be his penultimate appearance for the Blues and three weeks later he was wearing the red and white of Arsenal playing against Everton.

Terry Darracott: We played at Arsenal only two weeks after Alan Ball had left us and the boss informed me that my job was to man-mark him. I'd been called on to do similar jobs that year and had already gone one-on-one with George Best and Colin Bell. But Alan was a different type of challenge. He had been a great friend and had looked after me during my early days at the club. Although it was weird to see him dressed in red and white, I thought I'd better just get on with it and got stuck into him from the kick-off. Within minutes he responded and whacked me in my Adam's apple. I went down like a sack of spuds. Our trainer asked me what I was doing on the floor but I couldn't speak as I fought for my breath. It was less than a fortnight since we'd been team-mates but there was definitely no sentiment on his behalf.

Off the field ...

Team-mates had much in common in the late-sixties. They came from similar backgrounds, earned similar wages and socialised together.

Alex Young: For someone who hated defeat, I was surprised that Bally loved horse-racing. He found no shortage of company among his team-mates for his racing excursions, but I was responsible for introducing him to the heartaches of ownership when we bought a horse called 'Daxel'. Our two-year old was trained by Dickie Westbrook at the famous JF Watts stables in Newmarket. Bally and 'Daxel' - two thoroughbreds but only one of them was a winner.

Gordon West: I've never had a major bet on a horse in my life but many of the lads loved the gee-gees. Labby was serious about his horse-racing, his dad had done very well at it and even named his horse 'Goodison.' On one away trip, when he was injured and had stayed at home, we were driving through London when Harry Catterick asked: *"Is Labby's horse running today? Should we have a flutter?"* I replied: *"It's rubbish, boss. It'll come last!"* About an hour later we pulled up at some traffic lights opposite a betting shop and I spotted the freshly chalked sign in the window announced 'Winner - Goodison 25/1'. I kept a low profile for the rest of the day.

Colin Harvey: We were mostly about the same age and pretty good friends off the pitch. We didn't live in one another's pockets, but we'd congregate at the Bulldog pub near Bellefield after away trips. If there was a day out at the races I'd go, but I was never a gambling man.

Sandy Brown: I earned £50 a week during the 69/70 season and also got an end-of-season bonus of £2 for every game that I played in. It was good money but, with a wife and family at home, I'd to be careful when playing poker or three-card brag on the bus. Card schools have always been prevalent in the game and some players would lose their wages on the way to an away fixture and their win-bonus on the way back.

Brian Labone: Bally was on more money than the rest of us but, having said that, money never seemed to bother us. As professional footballers playing in the royal blue of Everton, we were happy with our lot. After all our red-haired star made things happen and earned every penny. We were paid on Thursdays and often would go to the races. I graduated from enthusiast to owner when I bought an unraced two-year old for the princely sum of £500. As the owner of 'Goodison', who won 10 races, I'd a little more luck than some of my team-mates. Alex and Bally had invested more heavily and were very proud of their thoroughbred, so much so, that they engaged a top horseman to ride their pride and joy at Haydock Park. The horse failed to make an impression and after the disappointing run Bally is alleged to have asked the jockey for his opinion of 'Daxel'. The horseman was a man of few words and responded: *"Glue!"*

Roger Kenyon: After a win we'd enjoy a laugh on the journey back to Merseyside. But if we'd been beaten, Catterick's icy glare guaranteed a very quiet coach ride home.

Ernie Horrigan: I drove the team coach during the glory years. It was a top-of-the-line Leyland Rapid - the first with a television and a giant rear-view mirror. Keith Newton would hog the back seat, Royle and Hurst would sit a few rows in front of him and the card sharks would occupy the seats around the tables. Husband liked to read. Wright and Kendall preferred to sit towards the front, not far from the boss who would always take the third row from the door with Wilf Dixon immediately in front of him. The directors would take their places half-way down the bus. There was always a buoyant mood on the way to the ground. And if we won - the lads were allowed a beer or two on the way home but on the rare occasions when we didn't win - it was like driving a hearse. I'd position my mirror to keep one eye on Mr Catterick.

Gordon West: We travelled to away games the day before but never got to see the sights, in fact we rarely went out of the hotel and we never had a drink. By the time we'd showered and had our meal, it was time for bed. Colin always roomed with Tommy and Howard shared with Bally. I roomed with Labby and we used to be given a little sleeping pill to ensure that we got a good night's kip. Wilf Dixon would bring the little red pills to our room. I realise now that he was checking up on us. Before going to bed at half-ten, we'd put our shoes outside the door and then go through our own little ceremony. We'd lie in our beds and say: *"Are you ready love?"* and then swallow the pills together like in a suicide pact. Labby would mumble: *"I'm fading."* The next thing I knew there'd be a knock on the door and it was my breakfast. The room-service waiter would also deliver our sparkling shoes. Maybe it's something to do with me being a Yorkshireman, but I used to leave at least four pairs outside my door!

Alan Ball: There was great camaraderie and we were a very close group of players. I was a bit of a wild thing in my early days at Goodison until Alex Young took me under his wing.

Tommy Jackson: I was in digs and knocked about with Roger Kenyon, Frank D'arcy and Terry Owen. Merseyside was a great place to be in the sixties and we all liked to wear the latest gear at the Beachcomber club. In contrast Jimmy Husband was a bit of a loner who used to wear all the psychedelic flower-power stuff. He also owned a babe-magnet - an E-type. I was very impressed with the life-style of the professional footballer and couldn't believe the grandeur of the facilities at Bellefield, particularly the car park full of exotic cars. That is until I caught sight of Andy Rankin parking his vehicle behind one of the buildings - it was a red Reliant Robin!

Jimmy Husband: Howard was a conscientious lad, or at least he was until Ernie Hunt, our unofficial social secretary, and Bally led him astray. The dressing room was divided by two factors - where you lived and your interest in golf. I think that only Colin, Alan Whittle and Tommy Wright were my neighbours in the Woolton area. Everyone else lived out towards Formby and in the days before motorways it wasn't too easy to get across the city. Ironically I only took up golf after retiring from football. I think my timing was flawed because if we'd enjoyed a good result 'The Catt' would reward us with either a day off or alternatively a round of golf at one of the first-class clubs around Southport. The golf would be generally followed by a slap-up meal. Without exception, I elected to take the days off and spent them with my blue beauty - my E-type Jag. Sadly she had to be sacrificed not long after I got married.

Frank D'arcy: I earned about £50 per week whereas Colin and Howard were on £70 and Bally was on about £150. Bally liked to take out a wad containing several hundred pounds from his pocket and brag that he'd beaten the bookies again. He would have bet on two flies climbing up the wall. None of us were big drinkers and I remember that one sweltering afternoon after training John Hurst, Colin Harvey and I popped into the Hanover for a soft drink, nothing stronger. By the following Tuesday 'The Catt' claimed to have received 20 letters from concerned supporters reporting our pre-match revelry in a public house. He docked £30 from our wages and advised us to find a watering hole outside of the city. The only incident involving excess alcohol that comes to mind was after 'The Holy Trinity' had over-run Arsenal on the opening day of the 69/70 season. Westie commandeered the two celebratory bottles of whisky and challenged Sandy Brown to consume the contents by the time we reached Merseyside. They glared at each other eyeball-to-eyeball as they gulped down their tipples. The duel was declared a draw but, as Sandy staggered off the coach, Westie confessed that he'd replaced the contents of his bottle with cold tea in London.

David Johnson: Bally and the rest of the lads were great fun to be around. In particular Westie was a larger-than-life character who also served as our union rep. He'd hold court at Bellefield and would even don a black-cap when passing sentence on the innocent and guilty alike.

Football League Division 1 - 1969/70

		home					away					
	W	D	L	F	A	W	D	L	F	A	Pts
1 Everton	17	3	1	44	19	12	5	4	26	15	66
2 Leeds United	15	4	2	50	19	6	11	4	34	30	57
3 Chelsea	13	7	1	36	18	8	6	7	34	32	55
4 Derby County	15	3	3	45	14	7	6	8	19	23	53
5 Liverpool	10	7	4	34	20	10	4	7	31	22	51
6 Coventry City	9	6	6	35	28	10	5	6	23	20	49
7 Newcastle United	14	2	5	42	16	3	11	7	15	19	47
8 Manchester United	8	9	4	37	27	6	8	7	29	34	45

Goodison Dreams

interviews with their team-mates

Poised to dominate English football

March 27-30, 1971

Aspects of the Ball deal will never be known

Poised to dominate English football ...

Everton had laid the foundations for a football dynasty but inexplicably the famed midfield trio managed one FA Cup final appearance and one League championship.

Tommy Wright: We certainly didn't realise our full potential. I can't put my finger on why, we just seemed to fade away. We were a very young side and should have been at our peak for at least another three seasons.

Howard Kendall: We should've picked up a couple of FA Cups as well as a few more League championships. Everyone had expected a free-scoring Wembley classic in 1968, but nothing could have been farther from the truth because both teams laboured through an unproductive 90 minutes. We were desperately disappointing on the day - there just wasn't an edge to us. We had plenty of opportunities to win without playing as well as we knew that we could but missed our chances. Whereas Jeff Astle didn't miss his. I was convinced that we were the best team in the country and took the line, the same as when we won in 1984, that the League title had to be our primary objective. After winning the 69/70 championship by 9 points, I was bitterly disappointed that our success didn't last another three or four seasons because the football we played was tremendous. It was attractive in the true Everton tradition. We served up some good stuff to win the title, then the following season suffered two big disappointments in a really cruel week which influenced Harry Catterick to change things. We were eliminated from the European Cup by Panathinaikos on the Wednesday and from the FA Cup by Liverpool on the Saturday. It all seemed to go wrong very quickly. Key players like Wilson, Morrissey and Labone were sidelined and, of course, there was Alan Ball's growing dissatisfaction. We had the best team until we started to break up. It was obvious that the replacements coming in were not of the standard of those going out.

Roger Kenyon: I also have difficulty coming to terms with what went wrong. Even though some of the lads were approaching the end of their careers, most were young and hungry and we should've dominated English football for years. Had we beaten Panathinaikos and Liverpool, who knows what we might have achieved in the following years. It could've been a royal blue dynasty.

Alex Young: The truly great managers are able to reproduce success season after season after season. Any team inspired by Kendall, Harvey & Ball should have won more honours. Perhaps the alarm bells were ringing at Wembley when we slipped on the West Bromwich banana skin. We'd played some magnificent football in that latter part of the season and enjoyed a strong run in the FA Cup. I'd come on as the sub in the semi-final and had played well. Immediately after the game the manager indicated that I'd have the same role at Wembley, but Roger Kenyon wore the No 12 shirt that day. We'd trounced West Brom in both League games and a lot of people were upset by the way that we lost the final. Many point to the ease of our victory at the Hawthorns but I can also recall the home game in October when I played wide right against a Wales international called Graham Williams. I could've put him in my pocket. He played in the final but I didn't.

Joe Royle: The challenges were pretty physical early on and the game just seemed to pass me by, but nevertheless we enjoyed the better of a dour contest and should have won the FA Cup in 1968. I was a 19-year old kid and was totally devastated by the result because everyone had fancied us to win quite comfortably. Of course, we recovered and matured into a very good championship-winning side before disintegrating immediately after the exits from the European Cup and the FA Cup in 1971. We all knew that a great era was over when Bally left and things began to crumble in his absence.

Jimmy Husband: My nightmare miss happened as the final was heading towards extra-time. The West Brom keeper, John Osborne, was stranded as the ball came over towards me. I knew that Bally was behind me and was in two minds whether to head the ball. As I rose I heard his distinctive voice: *"Leave it!"* Sadly the record books show that I fluffed the golden opportunity to take the FA Cup back to Goodison Park. Bally reacted angrily for a couple of seconds but then threw himself back into the game. He was a true professional and has never mentioned the incident to this day. I was only 20 and was distraught at losing at Wembley. Even though we were inexperienced, we knew that we were the far superior side. I vaguely remember collecting my runners-up medal from Princess Alexandra and entering our dressing room. All the heads were down - everyone was staring at the stud marks on the floor. But there was no ranting or throwing of crockery. We were too choked for that. I do recall Ray Wilson putting his arm around me and trying to console me: *"Don't worry Jim, it could have happened to any of us."* I don't lose sleep about the game but I do sometimes see that ball coming towards me. Of course I have never wanted to watch the video of the final, that would be like asking Goering to watch the Nuremberg Trials.

John Hurst: One championship - but there should have been so much more silverware in the Goodison trophy room. It wasn't over-confidence against West Brom in 1968. We had been in fine form but on that day at Wembley I think that we could have played for another two hours and not scored. The result proved to be the spring-board for the 69/70 title but sadly our reign was short. One reason for our subsequent decline was the inclusion of so many Everton representatives in the 1970 World Cup squad. Wright, Labone, Newton and Ball came straight back from Mexico exhausted, but as champions we were expected to dominate the League again. We started slowly and panic set in. The team was far from old, they just never gave the World Cup lads time to recover from their battle fatigue. The situation was further complicated by Harry Catterick's long spell of illness and by the absence of his trusted right-hand men, Wilf Dixon and Tommy Eggleston, who had moved on. Tommy Casey had taken over as trainer and had a different philosophy of football. He wanted us to belt the ball as far as we could. This was a joke to us because we used to take great pride in creating from the back. Casey would say: *"I only want you to have two touches, one to stop it and one to kick it."*

Ray Wilson: We should have beaten them 6-0. As a veteran in a young team, I found it very difficult to come to terms with our loss. The post-match dressing room was silent - just like there had been a death in the family. I'd enjoyed some magical moments at Wembley with Everton and England, but losing to West Brom was very painful.

Alan Ball: I've never seen a more one-sided FA Cup final where the better team lost. I couldn't believe how much possession we had. We seemed to play the game in their half and missed so many chances. The only thing we were really missing was a bit of luck.

Roger Kenyon: I had replaced John Hurst in the quarter-final and the semi-final, but he recovered from his jaundice complaint and was back in the line-up at Wembley. From the bench we looked the better side by far. Wilf Dixon asked me to warm up on a couple of occasions, but I didn't get on to the hallowed turf - not even in extra-time. I was only 19 and was very angry at losing the final. We had our opportunities, but just couldn't find the back of the net. Jimmy Husband had wasted several half-chances that he normally would have tucked away and was inconsolable in the dressing room. We were all responsible for not bringing home the cup and, in footballing terms, it was the saddest day in my life.

Sandy Brown: I watched from the sidelines and felt helpless by events unfolding on the Wembley turf. I consoled myself with the knowledge that we were a very young side and was convinced that we would be back in the near future. I never saw the twin towers again.

Gordon West: Although Kendall, Harvey & Ball were synonymous with cultured football, the team didn't perform well in the 70/71 season. I've the greatest respect for Bally as a player but in my opinion he ruined us and I was to blame! It all revolved around a through-ball at Turf Moor during the previous season. Steve Kindon, Labby and I went for it but, of course, there was only going to be one winner. Unfortunately I hit Labby in the kidneys and he had to miss the last eight games. Consequently, Bally was made captain for the run-in and we won almost every game. Catterick must have thought to himself:*"I'll keep him as skipper"* but it turned out to be one of the worst things that has ever happened to Everton.

Brian Labone: The boss always sold players before he thought that they were finished and loved to make a profit on all of his deals, so he tended to break up a side before it got too long in the tooth. He had broken up the 62/63 championship side which he'd inherited from Johnny Carey by selling Vernon, Parker and Bingham and did the same seven years later. But the major difference was that the 69/70 side was very young and should have gone on and on.

Keith Newton: The championship triumph should have been the start of a sparkling era for Everton, yet it never happened. Harry Catterick wasn't very good at capitalising on success.

Terry Darracott: By the time that I'd earned a decent run in the first-team, the core of the championship side had long gone and the glory days were over. Nevertheless, I was honoured to serve my apprenticeship in their company. My first job was to look after the kit in the first-team dressing room. I'd start work early in the morning when the gear would come back from the wash. It would be left in a big pile on the floor and I'd sort it into numbers, fold it and put it on the bench by their pegs. I used to clean Colin's and Bally's boots too and my claim to fame is that I've polished the ones he wore in the World Cup final. One of the best things about preparing the first-team dressing room was that I could listen to them all talking about everything and anything.

Frank D'arcy: Wilf Dixon and his predecessor Tommy Eggleston were football men who knew how to get the best out of the lads at Bellefield. On the other hand, Stuart Imlach, had few coaching ideas other than organising games of 5-a-side and Tommy Casey had no ideas at all. It's frightening to think that he was the caretaker manager when the boss was recovering from illness. Is it any wonder that our ambitions crumbled?

Billy Bingham: The club was fighting relegation when John Moores asked me take on the role of manager. I was only 42 and thought that it was a bit too soon but the blue blood in me couldn't resist the challenge. It was a massive job because I was replacing someone who had enjoyed a tremendous amount of success. He also proved to have a very large blue shadow. Alan Ball had already gone but I don't think that his transfer had been the turning point. Other key players were getting old. An average football career is about a dozen years and players are at their peak, both physically and mentally, for about half of them. The Everton midfield had been a great trio but had gradually faded. It was just the natural end of their playing lives. Howard Kendall was approaching 30 and had probably had his best days. The club had prospered during his playing days but personnel changes were required and I'd been recruited to make them. Obviously, they were a hard act to follow but my mission was to assemble a new midfield which could function as smoothly as their famous predecessors. I brought in Martin Dobson, Andy King and Bruce Rioch and improved the League standings every year. We were lying in mid-table when John Moores called me into his office: *"We are not going to win the League, are we Mr Bingham?"* I said: *"No, but we are in the semi-final of the League Cup and the fifth round of the FA Cup."* But he wasn't interested. To this day I can see Gordon Lee leading out my team at Wembley.

John Connolly: I arrived from the obscurity of St Johnstone a few months after Alan Ball had left. Everton were a massive club and had been poised to conquer Europe only 12 months earlier, but in retrospect were struggling through a period of major change involving the retirement of established stars and the introduction of new faces. The upheaval was also impacted by Catterick's poor health. We didn't see much of him and the day-to-day coaching was supervised by Stuart Imlach. But even though the championship-winning side and the legendary midfield unit had been broken up, there were still plenty of influential players around. Colin Harvey immediately caught my eye as a truly outstanding footballer despite his battle with an assortment of injuries. Howard Kendall was another very important player who effectively ran the engine-room. Everyone at the club liked him. It must have been very difficult for the new manager to even attempt to replace players of their calibre, nevertheless Billy Bingham tried hard to inflate the Everton dream. Unfortunately, my contributions were cut short by career-threatening injuries and after spending 12 months in the treatment room I was perhaps too impatient to seek first-team opportunities elsewhere. I realise now that I should never have left Goodison. I eventually teamed up again with Howard Kendall and Gary Jones at Birmingham. By then, Howard had slowed down a little but lost none of his ability.

Mick Buckley: I'd admired 'The Holy Trinity' from the sidelines for some time and eventually made my debut in March 1972. By that time the Everton dream was over and the club had plummeted to the lower reaches of the table. Our line-up for my baptism against Wolves included Peter Scott, John McLaughlin, Mike Lyons and Bernie Wright and I actually wore the No 8 shirt that had previously been the exclusive property of Alan Ball. Of course, I felt privileged to be in the same Everton team as Howard Kendall and the rest of the lads. My debut was a 2-2 thriller but turned out to be a real eye-opener for me. My lasting memory was of the respect that everyone on the pitch, including the officials, gave to Johnny Morrissey. It wasn't until half-time that I noticed Bernard Shaw, the England Under-23 defender, hobbling towards the tunnel. His legs were black and blue. His gold socks were in tatters and coloured red with his own blood. It was only then that I realised that the unfortunate right-back would had to endure another 45 minutes against the Goodison hard-case.

Len Capeling: Kendall, Harvey & Ball's finest hour? It was April Fools' Day 1970 but I didn't know whether to laugh or cry because I had pulled a muscle in my left leg celebrating Alan Whittle's opener against West Brom. After clinching the title by such a handsome margin, I had expected that we would pick up more silverware during the seven years remaining on Harry Catterick's contract and doubt if any one of the 60,000 crammed into Goodison Park that afternoon could have predicted that the club would descend into gloom within 12 months and that team would disintegrate within 24. The reasons often cited for the decline are that Ball's transfer ripped the heart out of the side and that Catterick's heart attack, shortly after that transaction, left the club rudderless for months. But I think that the fall from grace may also have been accelerated by a combination of several other factors. Because not long after the champagne bubbles had subsided, Goodison was besieged with problems related to the extra-curricular activities of several young, and not so young, players and team selection was undermined by chronic injuries to Royle and Harvey and the premature loss of Labone, Brown, and Morrissey. I must admit that I was never a big fan of the left-winger and had always thought of him as a tug-boat player with a bit of skill in his boots. He had been signed by Harry Catterick, who was a master at cloak and dagger swoops. Kendall, and Ball were also products of his dealings in the transfer market. Despite his failing health, the Everton manager toiled in vain to build another team. The struggle was too much for him and he moved to one side. Sadly the damage had been done and, some years later, I remember him fighting for his life at Goodison. He'd had a history of coronary problems and collapsed during the Ipswich Town cup tie in March 1985. The paramedics placed him on the roofs of the executive boxes in front of the Main Stand and frantically tried to revive him. It was a sad day for football.

March 27-30, 1971 ...

The pride of Goodison was dented by two significant defeats in three days. The reigning champions never recovered from the disappointments of Athens and Old Trafford.

Howard Kendall: Athens was a frightening experience. Their fans kept up a barrage of noise outside our hotel throughout the night before the game and we couldn't sleep. The stadium was a hostile environment. The crowd were caged in behind fences but would spit at us at every opportunity - especially when we went to take throw-ins. We ended up drawing 0-0, which was a tremendous result, but had been effectively eliminated at Goodison. What a tragic waste! Had we defeated Panathinaikos, we could have taken the most coveted of trophies back to Merseyside years before Liverpool managed to. I wasn't surprised when Ajax beat them 2-0 in the final, but it would have been a lot closer had Everton been there.

Colin Harvey: We'd set our sights on the European Cup at the expense of the domestic competitions. Sadly our ambitions came unstuck against Panathinaikos, who we'd thought were an easy quarter-final tie. We battered them at Goodison but couldn't get the goals we deserved. If only one of the shots that struck the woodwork had gone in, it could've changed the club's history. The Athens trip was an absolute nightmare. The hotel was on an island and the Greek fans made a racket all night long. Our misfortune peaked on match-day when we were subjected to several dubious refereeing decisions. We should've been awarded a blatant penalty when Alan Whittle was brought down near the penalty spot. When the ref gave an indirect free-kick, it dawned on me there was no way we were going to get anything out of the game. They went through on the away goals rule then beat Red Star Belgrade in the semi-final. I was one of the Everton party who picked up a bug in Greece. Harry Catterick was so ill that he was unable to attend the FA Cup semi-final on the Saturday. We played well for an hour at Old Trafford but lost 1-2. Those two defeats knocked the wind out of our sails.

Alan Ball: The Greeks were managed by Ferenc Puskas, who had been a truly world-class player, and had scraped a draw in the first-leg through a break-away goal. The gods or at least the Greek ones were against us in the second-leg. We were very unfortunate to draw 0-0 in Athens. I honestly believe that with a bit of luck we could've been in the European Cup final that year. The final was at Wembley and we could've gone all the way.

Frank D'arcy: The locals pelted our bus with rocks on the way to the ground. Fortunately their aim was crap, but they were far more deadly at spitting. I'd the misfortune to sit on the sub's bench throughout the 90 minutes and had first-hand experience of their disgusting accuracy. My tracksuit was covered with spit and rotten fruit and to make matters worse we were eliminated from the European Cup by an inferior team.

Roger Kenyon: Evertonians were planning for two big days out at Wembley. I played in the European Cup first-leg at Goodison and felt that we should have beaten Panathinaikos by six clear goals, but it was one of those days. Our posh hotel, the Aperghis in Kiffiscia was serenaded by a chorus of car horns all night and in the stadium we were subjected to a torrent of Greek phlegm. From my experience on the sub's bench, Panathinaikos fans were all heavy smokers who suffered from catarrh. The hysteria from being knocked out of Europe turned to unspeakable horror at Old Trafford. Wilf Dixon took charge of the preparations for the FA Cup semi-final and informed me that Sandy Brown would wear the No 12 shirt at Old Trafford. As it happened Labby was injured in the second-half and our weakened defence struggled to come to terms with the aerial tactics of Liverpool. We were all devastated by the two major setbacks in such quick succession. My mood after the game was not improved by Wilf Dixon's confession that perhaps the outcome was influenced by his choice of substitute.

Johnny Morrissey: We were apprehensive that the officials would be intimidated by the home crowd and didn't expect to get much out of the game in Athens. As 25,000 hostile Greeks bayed for our blood, the French referee underlined our worst fears. We didn't dwell on our exit from Europe and were confident of reaching the FA Cup final. Having kicked off my career at Anfield, I considered Merseyside derby games to be extra special and had enjoyed a great record against the Reds. In fact, everything was going to plan at Old Trafford until Labby went off. I suggested to Wilf Dixon, who had picked up the reins in Harry's absence, that we switch Big Joe to centre-half for the last half-hour. However my advice was ignored and Sandy struggled with their aerial bombardment. The defeat was a bitter pill and confirmed an old football adage - it's worse to lose a semi-final than a final and even more painful to lose a semi-final to your neighbours. I went straight home after the game and never gave a thought to going out for a drink. What would you order - arsenic?

David Johnson: I came on for Jimmy Husband at Goodison, equalised in the dying minutes, and also came on as substitute in the away leg. The atmosphere in Athens was intimidating. Their players treated the game as a spitting contest and I came off the pitch with my shirt dripping in the stuff. It was all part and parcel of European football.

Brian Labone: Les Shannon was with Salonika and Billy Bingham was managing the Greece national side at the time and they warned me that we were in for a sticky encounter. We played well but the no-score draw wasn't enough. I'd picked up a hamstring injury in Athens but looked forward to the challenge at Old Trafford. We were a much better team than the Reds - something that we demonstrated throughout the first-half. In fact I don't recall Andy Rankin being troubled by any of their efforts until after I'd aggravated my injury. I'd have been glad to soldier on if we hadn't had a utility player of Sandy Brown's quality on the bench. As it turned out, Liverpool scored from two ungainly lobs into the box. Afterwards, Westie and I drowned our sorrows at the Punch Bowl pub in Sefton. It was only then that we realised that we'd suffered the same fate as United had experienced back in 1966 and that we needed to pick ourselves up quickly. That proved to be a difficult task because I managed only half-a-dozen more outings before an Achilles injury forced my retirement.

Tommy Wright: We were confident that we'd bounce back and beat Liverpool. The game turned as soon as our leader limped off. To say the post-match mood in the dressing room was subdued is an understatement.

Brian Hall: Alun Evans crossed from the left, John Toshack challenged Andy Rankin and the ball was knocked down to me in the penalty area. I realised that Howard Kendall was on the line and decided to volley it early. At the time you don't think of the big picture, we were 2-1 up and there was a chance of going to Wembley. It was my first goal for Liverpool, the winning goal of the semi-final, and it was against Everton. It doesn't get much better than that!

Sandy Brown: I came on to mark John Toshack, who had springs in his boots that day. I told Tommy Wright that I needed help but he reassured me that I could shove Tosh into my pocket. When the red striker equalised I felt awful and when Brian Hall got their winner my world fell apart. Deep down I think we knew that it was all over. Even the supporters changed. They were too disappointed to speak to us. I played in three semi-finals and never got to play at Wembley.

Joe Royle: Our dreams evaporated within the space of 72 hours. Kendall, Harvey & Ball seemed to have recovered from our European set-back and played very well in the first-half at Old Trafford. Bally had put us in the lead but shortly after the break Labby went off with a hamstring injury and Sandy Brown moved to centre-half to take care of John Toshack. The Reds assumed control of a typically frenetic derby game and won through to Wembley. When referee Ken Burns blew the final-whistle it signalled the end for a great Everton side.

Aspects of the Ball deal will never be known ...

On December 22, 1971 Everton sold Alan Ball to Arsenal for a British record fee. The blue side of the Mersey were lost for words - well almost.

John Quinn: My friend worked for the Giro Bank and actually handled the Arsenal cheque. He said there was something a little odd about it. I can't exactly remember now, but I think that it contained an odd number of new pence in the total amount. That evening Granada showed Alan Ball on the train going down to London, his dad beside him. Ball senior was the only one to make a statement along the lines of *"one day the facts will all come out"* but of course they didn't. There was talk of his cut being used to pay his debts and that he himself had requested the transfer to get that much needed cash, but who knows?

Colin Harvey: I was shocked to learn that Bally was leaving. Although he wasn't playing as well as he could do, he was still the best post-war player ever to have worn an Everton shirt. The boss had a fortune to spend, but I wondered how we were going to surpass Alan Ball?

John Hurst: He went very suddenly. We were training when Norman Borrowdale, our physio, called out: *"Bally, the gaffer wants to see you."* Because he was the captain we assumed it was for a chat about tactics or opponents. We all used to go down to the local cafe and were having a cup of tea when Bally came in. He said that he was off to Arsenal but we didn't believe him. The next morning we discovered that not only was it true but he'd already gone. I was flabbergasted. He should have been a crucial part of the Everton set-up for years.

Jimmy Husband: We were weathering a period of indifferent form. The situation had become a little turbulent with the continued absence of the manager through ill health and some of the fans had become restless. I have no recollection that there had been speculation linking Bally with a move and was as shocked as everyone else when I heard the news on the radio.

Roger Kenyon: Harry Catterick off-loaded Bally because he felt he'd had the best out of him. What a tragic mistake! His transfer was shrouded in mystery and the manager was reported to have said: *"Aspects of the Ball deal will never be known."*

Alex Young: The championship team was young, except for one or two, but in no time Catterick had broken it up. The demise started with the sale of Bally. I believe that he was as surprised as anyone by the speed of the transaction and it must have been a heart-wrenching decision for him to leave. From all accounts, Goodison was never the same.

Howard Kendall: Before his disenchantment with the club began to set in, Alan was quite possibly the finest midfield player Everton has ever had. Although he never lost his stomach for a battle, things started to go wrong for him when his goals-per-game ratio began to fall and he could no longer cover the same enormous amount of ground that he used to. Alan took it upon himself to play deeper and as a result his 20 goals per season dried up. I don't believe that his decision to leave can be totally attributed to his increasingly strained relationship with Harry Catterick. After all there wasn't a first-team player at the club who hadn't had the occasional run-in with a manager for whom the tag 'enigma' was admirably suited. Alan and I were friends and as such I'd listen to his complaints. During the later stages he moaned a little more than usual and I knew that it would only be a matter of time before he would leave us. Everyone was disappointed at his departure and the fans, in particular, felt a sense of betrayal.

Mike Lyons: I just remember him coming down the stairs at Bellefield in tears. He told me: *"I've got to go to Arsenal!"*

Frank D'arcy: Our mood was made worse by the next wave of signings. The likes of Bernard, McLaughlin and Wright were no better than the lads in the Central League team. Bernie Wright was a strange character who never showered after training, he just put his clothes back on and went back to his digs. Who told the boss that 'Bernie the Bolt' was ready for the big time? It was a cruel and thoughtless practical joke!

Tommy Wright: His departure came completely out of the blue. I've heard the stories about him leaving because he needed to clear some debts, but nobody told us anything officially.

Graham Wilson: As the eyes and ears of John Moores at the club in the 1960s, I recall that the club benefactor preferred not to get involved in the private matters of players. When the Everton manager proposed to transfer his star asset, I was informed that the player was entitled to 5% of the fee under the Football League guidelines. As a result of the transaction, everyone appeared to get what they wanted - everyone except the Goodison fans.

Terry Darracott: There had been a few rumours that he might be going, but nobody paid much attention to them. In fact everybody was really astonished and upset on the day that he told us he was going to Highbury. He loved Everton, he still does, and none of us could believe it. I don't know the reason why he left, it happened so suddenly and was quite mysterious.

Brian Labone: I gave up the captaincy because I believed that he was going to be at the club for years to come. Of course that wasn't to be. There were plenty of rumours circulating about why we sold him. I don't know anything about money troubles, but I do know that Catterick made a profit of £100,000 after reaping six years of outstanding service from him. As the manager struggled to replace him, several new faces were introduced including Mick Bernard from Stoke who was converted into a full-back. Other big-money additions such as Rod Belfitt, Dave Lawson, Joe Harper and 'Bernie the Bolt' Wright weren't championship material by any stretch of the imagination.

Ernie Horrigan: I'd pick up the lads and take them to Bellefield. They'd park their cars on the streets around the Winslow pub and had to be on board the team coach by 9.50 am prompt. Of course there would always be the occasional straggler - usually Big Joe. The 10 minute drive along Queen's Drive was uneventful, that is until the morning of December 22. When we got to the training ground I was told to wait rather than return to Lawrenceson's depot at Moreton Road in Bootle. Wilf Dixon said: *"Don't go anywhere this morning - I may need you."* Twenty minutes later he returned to the coach accompanied by Alan Ball. There was tension in the air and I don't remember a word being uttered on the journey back to Goodison. As he got off the coach, Bally said: *"I think I've had it, Ernie. Where's the nearest phone box?"* I pointed him towards the ones on the opposite side of the road from the Blue House. Later that afternoon *The Echo* reported that he had been sold to Arsenal.

Alan Ball: I hadn't been firing on all cylinders for about a year and, without making excuses, was one of the first to have a career-threatening pelvic problem. I needed regular injections and couldn't lift my legs at times. It was hard to get up and down the pitch, but at 26 I was far from finished and continued to play top-flight football for another dozen years. I honestly didn't want to leave Everton and was sold to Arsenal purely and simply for business reasons. I arrived for training one morning and was told that Harry Catterick wanted to see me: *"Bertie Mee is in the next room and we've agreed a price."* I told him that I didn't want to go. He said: *"I've doubled my money. We've had six great years. You've done a fantastic job for me and Everton. It will be a great deal for you. Go and earn yourself a few quid."* I telephoned my father before talking to the Highbury manager. My dad said: *"Look Catterick straight in the eyes and ask him if he wants you to go."* I did and he did.

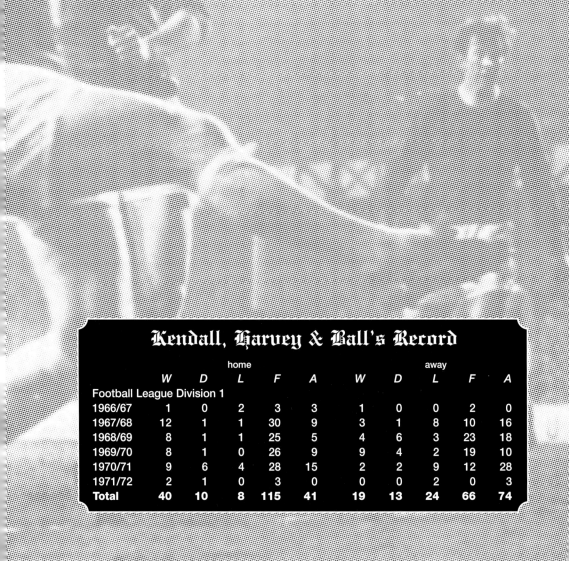

Kendall, Harvey & Ball's Record

	home					away				
	W	D	L	F	A	W	D	L	F	A
Football League Division 1										
1966/67	1	0	2	3	3	1	0	0	2	0
1967/68	12	1	1	30	9	3	1	8	10	16
1968/69	8	1	1	25	5	4	6	3	23	18
1969/70	8	1	0	26	9	9	4	2	19	10
1970/71	9	6	4	28	15	2	2	9	12	28
1971/72	2	1	0	3	0	0	0	2	0	3
Total	**40**	**10**	**8**	**115**	**41**	**19**	**13**	**24**	**66**	**74**

Gwladys Street's Adulation

recollections of their friends

School of Science memories

A reign too fleeting

They've sold Alan Ball

Blind admiration

School of Science memories ...

The quality of their football is legendary. Kendall, Harvey & Ball touched many lives - in many ways.

Gordon Watson: I played alongside some of the greatest stars of the game and I've no hesitation in saying that Kendall, Harvey & Ball wouldn't have been out of place with the likes of Bill Dean and Tommy Lawton. The midfield trio were honest players and would run their guts out for Everton. Ball was something special and was already a world-class player when he arrived. He had loads of self-confidence and could be very assertive. I think that he took our Latin motto to heart - and would play hell with his team-mates in training every now and then.

Neil Wolstenholme: I'm not sure how old I was when I first worked out that Kendall, Harvey & Ball were three people and not one, but I do remember my dad, a non-practicing Anglican not much given to catholic mysticism, proclaiming how wrong I was. KHB weren't simply three men, they were three-in-one. 'The Holy Trinity' were the perfect midfield. Individually fine players who, with the exception of Ball, were shamefully under-valued by Alf Ramsey, but who together transformed into a single seamless being which transcended mere team-work and took football to a new place. It was a land where elegance and beauty combined with power and delivery to achieve unity of purpose and total self-belief.

Graham Wilson: John Moores believed in employing people to do a job and not interfering. So Harry Catterick was given a free rein as well as an open cheque-book. Mr John didn't have favourites but I do recall that he had been particularly fond of Bobby Collins and, of course, Kendall, Harvey & Ball. He thought they were as good as he was ever likely to see. Three individuals who blended so well and seemed to spark each other. Ball had the heart of a lion and the pulse rate of a marathon runner. His only limitations were that he liked to take the Mickey out of opponents as well as argue with referees. Harvey was a tremendously talented player and for a handful of seasons when he was injury-free, he and George Best were the most gifted footballers in the country. Kendall was another cultured footballer. Although he didn't seem to graft as hard as his partners, he could pick out team-mates with his precise passing. They were three nice lads, but nice lads don't win much, and would have benefited from playing alongside someone who was prepared to put his foot in - like Tony Kay.

Len Capeling: They epitomised the School of Science. All three were fabulous players in their own right but their synergy resulted in an invincible union. Howard Kendall had it all - a hard tackler, a great distributor and one of the best strikers of a ball. Alan Ball was a real ball of fire. Sometimes his temperament let him down, but he bled when Everton lost and we all loved him for it. Although Colin Harvey didn't enjoy the popularity of Ball, he'd pirouette from challenges and glide across the pitch in a way reminiscent of 'Alex the Great'.

Mike Lyons: Before the infamous match at which Harry Catterick was reputed to have been attacked by some fans, my mate Frank Keagan and I bumped into Bally on a stretch of Blackpool's golden sands. The Sunday papers had linked him with several other top clubs and we pleaded with him to move to Everton. With so many clubs queuing up for his signature, perhaps our persuasive skills pushed him towards Goodison. Well I like to think it did.

Barry Hewitt: I'd get the train from Ipswich to London and then catch a football special to Lime Street. This service was intended for the visiting fans from Arsenal, Chelsea or Spurs and it was re-assuring for me to hear them express their respect for Kendall, Harvey & Ball and their fears about leaving Goodison Park empty-handed. Unfortunately, away trips soon became equally as unrewarding for Evertonians and we failed to record a single away victory during the 15 months before Ball left.

Phillip McNulty: There were no 'Dogs of War' at Goodison in those days. Ball was my hero and the focal point of a very good team. I was a 6-year old when I first caught sight of his ginger hair and white boots. There have been many influential Evertonians but he was the best to have worn a royal blue shirt. He was truly world-class and could pass exquisitely, tackle with intent and bag 20 goals a season. What would we give for an Alan Ball today?

John Keith: Harry Catterick was much maligned, after all he'd honed the sublime skills of Kendall, Harvey & Ball. In fact, his results were as good as those of any other manager in that era and his star should have shone brighter over Merseyside. He wasn't the best man-manager and could be ice-cold at times. Also he didn't interact very well with the press, sometimes misleading them. But he had a keen eye for talent and a refined nose for a deal. The Everton boss was an expert at cloak and dagger deals and through these transactions he assembled a beautifully balanced midfield unit. Ball was the dynamo, Harvey was the passer with slide-rule precision and Kendall provided great vision and industry. Driven by these tremendously talented players, Everton reached their zenith in 68/69 and 69/70 and then fell to pieces.

Tommy Jones: Ball had tremendous natural ability and was one of 10 world-class players ever to have played for the club. I helped Tommy Eggleston to introduce a rigorous training programme at Bellefield and remember that Ball wanted to beat every one at every exercise. He could recover from a state of near-exhaustion quicker than any other athlete that I've ever known. Ball played some 250 games and sweated blue blood in every one of them. His work ethic rubbed off on his team-mates. Kendall also had a brilliant football brain and Harvey was quick enough to catch pigeons. They dovetailed perfectly and were the best midfield unit of their era. They didn't have the bite of Bremner and Giles but were far more effective.

Stewart Imlach: I remember the 1969 derby game when Liverpool beat us 0-3 at Goodison, it was the game when Sandy Brown headed into his own goal. I'll never forget the scenes in the dressing room after the final-whistle. There was a deadly hush until Bally walked in. He picked up a cup of tea, walked to his bench, smashed the cup against the wall and set about berating his team-mates. Such was the loyalty to him that nobody said a word.

Gary Jones: Their party was over by the time that I'd broken into the first-team. But I do recall that their combined talents were even more effective than those of Giles and Bremner at Leeds and dominated the League for three seasons. Their sole weakness was their limited availability. I believe that their dynamic style of play caused above average wear and tear and, as a consequence, they managed to fulfil only 60% of fixtures as a trio.

Mick Buckley: It's something of a tradition for Everton juniors to rush over to Goodison and catch the final 20 minutes of first-team games. From my recollections of these excursions, Kendall, Harvey & Ball appeared to mesmerise visitors. The manager liked to blood youngsters in first-team training sessions and when it was my turn I found the experience to be nerve-racking. Bally had it all and I deeply regret never having had the opportunity to play with him in a competitive game. But I was privileged to have turned out alongside Howard and Colin.

Dave Hickson: We had waited 30 years for them. Of course the game had changed a lot during that time but Kendall, Harvey & Ball displayed a level of creativity similar to that of Britton and Mercer. Sceptics cite their modest haul of honours, but sometimes greatness can't be measured in silver. They may have won relatively few trophies, but they won many friends.

George Hogan: Ball had a rugged confidence in his own abilities - something that had been instilled into him as a child. When his father was the manager at Ashton United in the Lancashire Combination, he threw his son into the first-team. Alan was 14 but looked only 10.

Bill Kenwright: I was at the bar in Jimmy Ireland's night-club when someone tapped me on the shoulder: *"Don't you play Gordon Clegg in Coronation Street? I'm a big fan of yours!"* It was Colin Harvey and I was so in awe at meeting him in person that I was speechless. I honestly believe it's of the only times in my life when I've been lost for words.

David Kennedy: As a schoolboy exiled in Durham, I'd hitch-hike to Everton games. Like many young fans, I idolised Alan Ball. In particular, I recall a League Cup tie against Sunderland. I'd no difficulty in getting a lift to Goodison and was delighted by the ease at which Alex Young gave us a 2-0 lead. Unfortunately Kendall, Harvey & Ball eased their grip and Sunderland fought back to level terms. Just before the end, Everton were awarded a penalty and my hero took the kick and hit the post. As I contemplated the long journey back to the North East, bad turned to worse and the visitors grabbed the winner. I was totally devastated and decided to avoid the Roker traffic on the roads, preferring to take the train. However without sufficient funds for a ticket I had to hide in the mail van. Among all the bags, I cursed Alan Ball under my breath. At York station I jumped on to the Darlington train. Throughout my journey I braced myself for the taunts of my school-mates and cursed the goal post. Finally, I reached home in time for school, but by then I was worshipping Alan Ball again.

Derek Hatton: It had been a memorable evening - the noise deafening and the atmosphere electric - and I'd the honour of introducing the last of the inductees into Gwladys Street's Hall of Fame. The big finish had been saved for Howard Kendall who had flown in from Greece. Only nine months earlier he'd been booted out of Goodison as a reward for keeping us in the top flight and the Hall of Fame celebrations were the first opportunity for the fans to express their appreciation to him. Well, I never even got the chance to mention his name during my introduction. I got as far as referring to him as *"one-third of The Holy Trinity and indisputably the club's most successful manager ..."* when the Adelphi simply erupted. His 600 fellow bluebloods went wild and seemed to carry their hero across the packed banqueting hall to the stage. It was one of those magical evenings that fans will talk about for years to come.

Phil Pellow: If you could have an amalgam of the three, you'd have the greatest midfielder of all time. Howard Kendall could always find space and liked to ghost into the box from nowhere. Colin Harvey, whose baby face masked his aggression, was all left foot. His pace was deceptive in that he was slower than he looked but when the other two went charging off on a sortie, more often than not, the ball would come back to Harvey. He had the same knack for anticipating play as Kevin Ratcliffe. Alan Ball was a tremendous player but a shite captain. He took over when Labone got injured and consequently the team spirit fell apart. It was Gordon West's fault because he careered into our star centre-half at Burnley and ruled him out for the remainder of that season. I think a lot of the younger players disliked Ball because every time he made a mistake, he'd scream at them in front of the crowd.

Brian Tottey: I'd pestered my dad to take me to Panathinaikos. The package from Speke was advertised for £30, which was a lot of money back then. Of course, I didn't get to go to Greece and gladly settled for Kendall, Harvey & Ball against George Best a few weeks later. United were in the bottom-half of the table and if you stopped Best, you stopped United. He was the Footballer of the Year at home and in Europe but looked second best against Harvey. Our superstar had just been capped by England and over-shadowed him both in skill and effort. He was quicker to the ball and seemed to want it much more than his Old Trafford counterpart.

Paul Rigby: My dad took me into the front row of the main stand for my birthday and I got to witness the magic of 'The Holy Trinity'. He sat back in his seat, re-lit his pipe and said: *"Ignore the other 19 and just watch Kendall, Harvey & Ball in action - we may never see their likes again."* As usual, he was right!

Steven Milne: I first questioned the existence of God when my father took me to Wembley in May 1968. I was just nine and it was my first visit to London. Before the big game we went sightseeing at Buck House, Parliament and St Paul's. The cathedral was packed with foreigners, including a group from West Brom. One of those Brummies cut an imposing figure. From behind his beer belly he smirked at my home-made rosette. He laughed, walked towards the altar, lit a candle, closed his eyes and mumbled a few words. My dad said: "*It's time to go! Our next stop is Wembley!*" I asked him to wait a minute because I also needed to say a prayer. Nervously I approached the altar. I picked up a long, white candle, lit it, and placed it prominently in front of the other candles. I knelt on the step in front of the altar and prayed: "*God if you really exist, please let Alan Ball score the winning goal this afternoon.*" With hope in my heart I glanced over my shoulder to check where my dad was standing, leaned forward, closed my eyes and blew out the WBA flame.

Eric Jones: My experiences have ranged from Dixie in Division 2 football to Big Dunc in the Premiership. During those years, we've fielded some excellent footballers in the middle of the park and without doubt the best were Kendall, Harvey & Ball. They were truly great players and the club was very fortunate to have the three of them at Goodison at the same time. I should add that Joe Mercer and Peter Reid wouldn't have been out of place in their company, but Kendall, Harvey & Ball had a unique chemistry. Great football skills and tremendous football brains - they always knew what to do with the ball. Harvey was sharp on the ball and Kendall read the game well. Alan Ball? People often cite his industry but he had much more to offer. His skills and his football savvy allowed him extra time to distribute the ball effectively. He was so influential that his transfer left the club in the wilderness for years.

Len Capeling: I listened to the BBC World Service commentary of the 1968 final in Australia. The radio crackled for two hours but Ball and company served up no joy. We created numerous chances yet Jimmy Husband declined to accept them. With hindsight Alex Young, who had appeared in the semi-final, may have been a more productive choice.

Gordon Lee: They were the best midfield combination that we've ever had and probably the best we'll ever see. Their hallmark was that they just knew where they were going to put the ball before they received it - they had great football brains and awareness and as soon as the ball went to any of them, they knew where it would end up. Talented players don't always work too hard but the three of them did and it transformed them into truly great players. Alan Ball was also an inspirational leader who could create chances, score goals, defend when not in possession and be the big engine in every game. He was a shining example that even little ones can become world-class players.

Jon Berman: The royal blue trio were the best in the game but never got the plaudits they deserved. In particular, Alan Ball has never been fully appreciated outside of his native North West but was the ultimate hero as far as the Goodison fans were concerned. The three of them worked so well together that the 69/70 championship team were la creme de la creme akin to the Manchester United of today. To see Kendall, Harvey & Ball week in, week out was fabulous and is one of the reasons why Everton fans are never satisfied. We still talk about them with such great affection because there's never been another midfield like them. Howard's spectacular goals from outside the box are sometimes featured on old videos. In fact I'm on one of them, I'm the little kid dancing up and down in a sheepskin coat.

Frank Hargreaves: True football fans revered Colin Harvey and his critics were forced to meet after dark, because it was a profanity to take his name in vain. Then the foundations of Goodison Park were rocked by his transfer to Sheffield Wednesday. It was a bolt out of the blue. One banner read: "*£70,000 is an insult to Colin Harvey - The White Pele.*"

John Dwyer: Because money was tight, my brother and I used to thumb a lift to home games. Our favourite vantage point was the grass verge at the junction of Townsend Avenue and the East Lancs Road. When the cars pulled up at the lights, we would simply throw ourselves upon the mercy of the drivers destined for Goodison. I remember one Saturday towards the start of the season when I approached a top-of-the-line car purring at the lights. I bent down at the driver's window making sure not to damage the very expensive paint-work: *"Any chance of a lift?"* The driver wound down his window and replied: *"Sorry son, I'm full up today."* I immediately recognised the voice of my hero. It was Alan Ball. Sadly there were five or six kids - all draped in blue and white scarves - already crammed into his luxurious leather upholstery.

George Orr: The media attention given to the triumvirate and the headline-stealing actions of Alan Ball often over-shadowed the performances of their Everton team-mates as well as their predecessors. By comparison, Gabriel, Stevens and Kay went about winning the 62/63 crown with little fanfare. Of course they had two world-beaters up-front in Alex Young and Roy Vernon to add the finishing touches. In particular, Jimmy Gabriel was an unsung hero - a Braveheart who had blue blood in his veins. His replacement, Howard Kendall, was a skilful player who only came into his element after Ball had left and his inspirational performances stabilised the club in the early-1970s. He was a colourful character who you either loved or hated. A big-game player whose unbridled passion often turned into indiscipline. I remember him tangling with Tommy Jackson in a practice match at Goodison and also confronting Howard Kendall at the Baseball Ground. His midfield partner had made his only bad pass of the game but Ball was quick to demonstrate his frustrations. It was his last game for Everton.

Brendan Connolly: Football fans can be somewhat insular and Evertonians are no exception. We like to put our heroes on pedestals. From all accounts, William Ralph Dean was one of a kind - famed beyond the boundaries of football. Also Joe Mercer and Tommy Lawton were genuine superstars. Kendall, Harvey & Ball deserve similar recognition because they were as good as any midfield unit that the game has known. I remember them playing in front of the partially demolished Goodison Road stand and feeling that the building site seemed an inappropriate setting for such cultured players. Ball was a household name but the Southern media marginalised the contributions of both Harvey and Kendall. How could they justify Welle of Chelsea, Storey of Arsenal, Viljoen of Ipswich, Perryman of Spurs and even Venables playing for England at the expense of Everton's gifted duo?

Jim King: Some clubs build their teams around a powerhouse midfielder. Everton were very special because we had three of them who dovetailed into a truly dominating unit. During their heyday in the late-sixties, their combined skills, industry and understanding were second to none. They even overcame the loss of rhythm associated with Colin Harvey's injuries to romp away with the 69/70 League championship without breaking into a sweat.

Dave Roberts: Evertonians have always worshipped icons like 'The Holy Trinity', but only time will confirm their rightful place in the club's proud history. Ball was an entertainer who needed to be noticed and his red hair and matching freckles never stopped glowing for the full 90 minutes. His side-kicks were less conspicuous to the untrained eye, but deserved equal billing at the Goodison shrine. I couldn't begin to describe how well they played.

Mike Kenrick: It was a match against Manchester City in 1967 and I was perched at the back of the old Goodison Road stand where only the pigeons had a better view. Way below me on that beautiful swathe, Ball skipped down the right-wing looking like he was preparing to cross to Joe Royle. Then he suddenly arrowed the ball a good 25 yards into the back of the Park End net. I don't know what it is about that goal, no-one else ever mentions it, but to me it captured the unequalled brilliance that was Alan Ball in a royal blue shirt.

Neville Smith: Bubbling Bally, the heir to the throne of Alex Young, was the inspiration behind a very good Everton side. He was idolised at Goodison and hated at Anfield. Perhaps once in a generation midfield chemistry clicks and in the sixties it came together at Everton. Bally along with Howard Kendall and Colin Harvey were the most formidable and stylish midfield unit in the League. Their strength came from their complementary qualities. Traditionally successful teams have a worker, a spreader and a cruncher. Everton's triumvirate offered much more. Ball and Harvey were buzzers with great ball skills. Ball and Kendall were great passers. Kendall and Harvey were fierce tacklers, but never ill-disciplined crunchers. As a bonus, Ball was a match-winner. It is inexplicable that Harvey and Kendall were virtually ignored by their country. In fact all three should have been picked for England as a unit.

Charlie Hengler: There was something special about them. They injected a certain pride into all Everton fans. Although I never liked Ball's arrogance, such as when he sat on the ball in a European Cup match, I adored his passionate performances against the Reds. Who could forget the FA Cup tie at Goodison which was also screened at Anfield? After he'd smacked the winner past Tommy Lawrence - 'The Flying Pig', I recall walking on air from the Gwladys Street terraces down Scottie Road to the Mersey Tunnel and then thumbing it to Ellesmere Port. I had no difficulty getting a lift because it seemed like most of the 100,000 plus spectators were heading in the same direction. In those good old traffic jams, there was no segregation of Ball's fans from his foes and you'd see both smiles and tears in the same car.

Norman Dainty: I've watched Everton throughout my life and can even remember Dixie Dean heading his record-breaking sixtieth goal. We've also been blessed with some outstanding players across the middle of the field, Joe Mercer, Cliff Britton and most recently Peter Reid had comparable talents, but Kendall, Harvey & Ball were truly exceptional. Much credit must go to Harry Catterick for bringing them together. Harvey had brilliant ball control and passing skills and Kendall was a tenacious worker who was always good for a goal. Ball was a class act who covered every inch of the pitch for Everton and his country. Also Johnny Morrissey, a much under-rated player, could help out in midfield when needed.

Ronnie Goodlass: Because of the flamboyant skills of Kendall, Harvey & Ball, most of their team-mates never got the accolades they deserved. Joe Royle had two good feet and even better balance, but wasn't worshipped like previous No 9s of his calibre. The same goes for Labby who was much better than Jack Charlton but only got 26 caps. Johnny Morrissey put the fear of God into defenders and should have played for England. Jimmy Husband was another exciting winger as well as a bit of an eccentric. He was one of the smokers and was a genuine blast from the past with his flowered shirts and his fancy sports car, I wouldn't say he wore freaky clothes but I don't think he would have ever got knocked down in the dark. Now I think about it he was like a cross between Graham Le Saux and Austin Powers.

Brian Snagg: It was the battle of the decade. Not Liston versus Clay or Tyson versus Holyfield, but Alan Ball from Farnworth versus Tommy Jackson from Belfast. The venue was Goodison Park and the occasion was the 1970 public practice match involving the Blues against the Ambers. I recall that Ball had the reigning League champions in his corner whereas Jackson had the likes of Sandy Brown, Roger Kenyon, Terry Darracott, Dave Johnson, Gary Jones and Harry Bennett at his side. The result was a bruising public spectacle and there was to be no re-match. In fact, there has never been a public practice match at Goodison since.

Brian Birchall: Alan Ball was the best Everton and England player since Dixie Dean. Without question, he was the best midfield player of all time and his wonderful technique made the game look so easy. Like Dixie, he didn't know the meaning of defeat. He loved to torture the Reds and had something else in common with Dixie - the Kop feared him.

Noel Gornell: Alan Ball has always had the gift to lift people. Anyone who has ever heard his after-dinner speeches couldn't fail to be stirred by his passion. He also has the uncommon ability to laugh at himself. I remember back in 1970, he concluded one speech: *"I've three wishes - for Everton to win the European Cup, for England to retain the World Cup in Mexico and for my voice to break before I'm invited to address you again."*

Frank D'arcy: Harry Catterick was ruthless with anyone who dared to cross him. After the game at Keflavik, we drove straight to the airport in order to catch the 10 pm flight back to Speke. When the bus stopped to refuel on the way, Michael Charters used the opportunity to phone his match report to *The Echo*. Even though Catterick noted that the respected sports reporter was still in the phone box, he ordered the driver to carry on to the airport. He shouted: *"Drive on! We're not waiting for the likes of him!"* Charters had to get a taxi back to the hotel and catch another flight the next day. He was even hard on Tony Kay. The manager washed his hands of his friend after he'd been fingered by *The People*. Catterick isolated his friend from the first-team squad and instructed him to train with the kids.

Tony Waiters: I came across Alan Ball for the first time when he was an apprentice sweeping the dressing rooms at Blackpool, He was a puny kid and my first impression was that he would never make the grade. But I was soon to discover that there was something very special about him. He wasn't a natural, but his determination to succeed made him a player of world stature

Neville Smith: Bill Shankly loved to talk about football for hours but hated to mention his neighbours. The Liverpool boss took great pride in the fact that he had prevented Denis Law from joining Everton during his spell in charge at Huddersfield Town. One day I asked him which Everton player he would like to sign, if he had the choice. Howard Kendall? Colin Harvey? Alan Ball? Shanks retorted: *"Sandy Brown."* He was dead serious.

Mike Lyons: 'The Catt' was the only manager I ever knew who had creases in his tracksuit. His office windows were at right-angles and he'd monitor the A-team from one and the B-team from the other. He ruled with an iron fist and struck fear into everyone's heart when he watched us. I remember one particular mid-week game against Bolton Reserves when we were undefeated at the top of the Central League. The boss showed up unannounced and some of the lads went to pieces. We got thrashed about 1-5.

Ronnie Goodlass: I was brought up an Evertonian, my grandfather and father were season ticket holders, and were at both of the Panathinaikos games. I can confirm that we had no luck in either of the legs. I was disappointed but ill-prepared for the further distress of losing to the Reds. Everything was hunky dory at half-time but then in next to no time it was 1-2 and we were left empty-handed. Even though Andy Rankin was at fault for the second goal, Lady Luck deserted the blue side of the Mersey yet again, You're born an Evertonian and that's the way you stay but it can be hard work at times. I don't think we've had any luck in the last 100 years. Any loss to Liverpool is painful but defeats in FA Cup semi-finals are simply horrendous. To this day the mere thought of Clive Thomas makes foam at the mouth. Of course, there were no foreign players back then and Merseyside derby games were notoriously hard fought. Looking at how referees flash yellow cards about nowadays, there wouldn't have been a player left on the pitch. Derbies were about passion and commitment and I think that's one of the reasons why the supporters still remember the Kendall, Harvey & Ball era with such reverence.

Roger Kenyon: I progressed through the ranks at Everton and came across some real characters during my time at the club. For example Harry Bennett, a local lad who played in a couple of first-team games during 1968, always took nine spoons of sugar in his tea.

Ernie Horrigan: There would always be a crowd of young Everton fans searching for tickets. Many of them had hitchhiked for hours and couldn't afford the price of admission. I remember our trip to Filbert Street in that miserable November just before Bally went south. One of my jobs was to gather up the excess comps from the players and distribute them to these young fans. As players like Labby, Bally and Westie left the coach they would willingly donate their spare tickets. The demand had out-stripped the supply at Leicester and I felt really sorry for three Evertonians left shivering and ticketless. So I approached the one remaining straggler, as he was about to leave the coach. I had better not mention his name. *"Do you have any comps for three kids?"* He glared at me and replied: *"Listen! I've got no tickets!"* Before locking the coach, I'd make sure that nothing had been left behind. And to my horror I discovered the discarded remains of nine tickets. They had been ripped into pieces and stuffed down the back of the seat where this player had been sitting!

Stephen Hickson: With quality like Kendall, Harvey & Ball in the side, Everton could afford to maintain the School of Science emphasis on quality football. Ball was a winner and, above all else, an Evertonian. He was the initial reason for my fortnightly pilgrimages from Carlisle to Goodison and chatting about our royal blue hero made the long post-match journey up the M6 fly by. He got me hooked on the Blues and is responsible for bringing so much joy into my life. More recently, there have been times when I could have strangled him for my addiction!

Tom Cannon: Howard Kendall is the only person qualified to be enshrined in Gwladys Street's Hall of Fame as a player and as a manager. In both capacities, he transformed the club's expectations and beliefs into glittering prizes and should be honoured for the great success that he brought to Goodison Park.

Derek Temple: I was privileged to witness the baptisms of all three of them. I was in the side for Colin's dramatic debut at Inter-Milan and for Alan's equally sensational introduction at Fulham. But I missed Howard's first game against Southampton, which from all accounts was less memorable. I did play alongside him against Spurs four days later but sadly it was another off-day and another 0-1 home defeat.

Bill Kenwright: My favourite memory of Alan Ball is his winner in the FA Cup victory over the Reds in 1967. The city was captivated by the excitement of the fifth round tie which pitted the cup-holders against the reigning champions and, with everyone wanting to see the game, tickets were changing hands at Wembley prices. There was a full-house at Goodison and at Anfield where another 40,000 followed the action on closed-circuit television. My uncle and I watched the game from the Bullens Road Paddock and we were on our tip-toes throughout the full 90 minutes. The ground erupted when Bally out-paced Ron Yeats, Tommy Smith and Tommy Lawrence to a loose ball and hit the sweetest of volleys into the Gwladys Street net. It was a memorable goal - a goal in a million from the man who on the day wore his black boots!

Roger Long: He couldn't hit long raking passes like Colin Harvey or crack spectacular goals like Howard Kendall. He couldn't waltz past defenders like 'The Golden Vision' or bullet headers like Big Joe Royle. He couldn't convert penalties like Roy Vernon or even be relied upon to control his temper like 'The Last of the Corinthians'. But Alan Ball was priceless to Everton. He was worth more to his club than any other player in the country.

John Collings: It was a pleasure to make the 400-mile trek to see Kendall, Harvey & Ball and we'd talk about their exploits for hours on the trip back to London. Their skills, industry and consistency made them the best midfield of their era, more gifted than Bremner and Giles. Ball would cover every blade of grass and his partners were never far behind him.

Wally Fielding: I've had the pleasure of meeting both father and son. I played against Alan Ball Senior when he turned out for Southport against Everton in the Liverpool Senior Cup. He was a tough customer who knew how to look after himself. In contrast, his son was one of the all-time greats of the English game. Perhaps he will never receive the credit that he deserved for his part in 1966, but I reckon if it hadn't had been for his immense contributions throughout extra-time then the likes of Hurst, Charlton and Moore would never have been knighted. Alan Ball Junior was my kind of player and seemed to exhibit a World Cup level of commitment every time that he pulled on the royal blue of Everton. He was much more than an unselfish work-horse - he was a brilliant footballer. I bumped into him a couple of years ago when he was managing Exeter City and I was scouting for Spurs. I introduced myself: *"Alan, I played over 400 times for the Blues and also played against your dad. Do you know who I am?"* He glanced at me and, as he turned to walk away, proclaimed: *"I've no fucking idea."*

Pete Warner: Alan Ball was the guest speaker at a sportsman's dinner in Bristol. After the meal I felt it only right that I should introduce myself to him. So dressed in my full black-tie regalia, I sauntered nervously towards him: *"Hello Alan, I remember you playing for Everton all those years ago. I remember how sad I was when you left and went to Arsenal."* I then took off my dinner jacket, rolled up my shirt-sleeve and showed him the Everton crest tattooed on my upper arm. He was totally unimpressed, but did say that his happiest playing memories were at Goodison. After he'd signed my menu, I wandered away, slightly dazed and feeling as if I was a teenager again. Nobody else could understand why I was so excited and humming: *"He's here, he's there, he's every fucking where Alan Ball, Alan Ball."*

Elizabeth France: I've lived with Alan James Ball for more than 30 years but have never met the man. My husband told me all about him on our first date and it was like listening to the mantra of a religious zealot. Knowing that I was a Farnworth lass, I suspected he thought that I must be related to his Everton hero. During my subsequent period of indoctrination I've been led to believe that there was a spiritual aura about Gwladys Street's favourite son. Fortunately I'd never questioned my husband's faith because a couple of years ago Alex Young told me that Ball was indeed the best player that he had ever seen. And gods don't lie, do they!

Tony Dove: Harry Catterick was a man of few words but I remember his sheer delight at snatching one particular player from under the nose of his arch-rival. But even the master at wheeling and dealing couldn't have predicted the impact of his initiative on the club's fortunes. He boasted in the matchday programme shortly after he'd closed the deal: *"When Mr Moores engaged me in 1961, he demanded that I get only the best for Everton. I knew from my long association with the club that only the best was good enough. I have made a bid for the best and am certain that is what I have secured, including my latest acquisition - Howard Kendall."* The No 4 was an old-fashioned right-half who was less active than the other two blue-arsed flies in the Everton midfield. But his manager sometimes gave the impression that Kendall didn't have the stamina to last the full 90 minutes, unlike say Colin Bell at Manchester City, and probably undermined his player's chances with England.

David Cairns: I was much too young then to take in any conspiracy type stuff regarding the transfer money but I've made up for it since! How did it all fall apart? Not enough of the cash went on the stadium and building for the future and too much went on poor players. Careers ended too early through injury. Poor managers and coaches who had no respect from the players - step forward Messrs Bingham and Lee, the start of the lads' culture, and what of the racist issues? They hold no water now, but did they then? I think we were too insular. The local talent of proud and staunch Blues dried up. How can you criticise Mike Lyons? But how many past Everton sides would he have played for?

Heather Woltz: On discovering that his mother, a life-long believer in 'The Holy Trinity', had been diagnosed with a terminal condition, my friend sought to do something special for her before she passed away. He contacted Everton and was thrilled when the secretary Jim Greenwood invited her to be a guest of the club at the next home game. They reported to the main reception at Goodison Park for a guided tour of the stadium which concluded in the home dressing room just as the players were assembling for the game against Arsenal. At that point Howard Kendall took up the role of host and personally introduced his players to her. She chatted with Ratcliffe, Sheedy, Southall and Steven and was impressed by their patience, good humour and youthful acne as well as the presence of a bottle of whisky on the physio's table. Their exchanges were more than hand-shakes and scribbled autographs on the back of the matchday programme and for the next half-hour the Everton manager treated her like one of his own family and reminisced about life in the coal-mining communities of the North East. As the kick-off approached, he whispered to her: *"You'll have to take your seat in the stands now because the lads are too shy to take their clothes off in front of you."* Before leaving she asked one special favour: *"Kevin Sheedy is my favourite, can you make sure that he scores today."* Howard Kendall promised: *"Our second goal will be dedicated to you."* Colin Harvey added: *"It will have your name written on it."* My friend's mother died a few months later and as it turned out Gary Lineker scored the second goal in the 6-1 destruction of the Gunners.

Ed Loftus: Harvey and Husband opened the Summer Fayre at Anfield Comprehensive School. I decided to follow them around to the rifle range. The targets were on wires which could be wound closer and closer towards the sharp-shooters. As Colin's target approached him, I asked for his autograph. He grabbed my pencil and stuck it in the bull's-eye before showing his target to Jimmy, who fell for it. I was so proud I'd been included in his joke.

Len Capeling: Catterick's youngsters peaked in the 68/69 season and should have walked away with the championship. Unfortunately, they threw away vital points in drawing five home games and 10 away games and failed to grasp the title. Most of their goals came from the exciting spearhead of Joe Royle and Jimmy Husband, both products of the club's incubator. 'Skippy' was a beautifully balanced yet unorthodox forward who was destined for greatness until he lost confidence after being clattered in a savage tackle by Dave MacKay and after missing a couple of goal-scoring chances to win the FA Cup in 1968.

Ian Bedford: I'd queued up for over two hours outside the Liverpool Stadium to buy a ticket for a Merseyside derby but the crush was a bit too rough so I decided to leave it. On the day of the match, I decided to go to Goodison Park to see if there were any touts outside the ground. If not, I planned to stand outside and listen to the roars. I arrived just before the kick-off and found a man with a spare who wanted face value for it. My good fortune peaked when Alan Ball scored in the Gwladys Street end, he was wearing his magic white boots.

Jessie Milne: I spent all of my working life in the offices at Goodison and have seen them all come and go. Harry Catterick was an austere man who wouldn't tolerate any nonsense from the staff or the players. He was very formal and would always address me as Miss Milne. He showed no hint of favouritism towards any of the players but was better liked by those who had been at the club as juniors. They were a well-behaved group of young men and I found Brian Labone and Colin Harvey to be real gentlemen. I remember bumping into Colin at the Astoria Hotel after we had won the cup in 1966. The sheer delight of the day had illuminated him, he was glowing and seemed to be at least two feet taller than when I'd seen him earlier.

Kevin Ratcliffe: Alan Ball was my hero and I worshipped him from the Goodison Road terraces. I don't think that I was attracted to his flame hair, his fiery temper or his white boots - it was his enthusiasm that caught my imagination.

Eileen Downey: Without knowing it, I've lived with Colin Harvey for the best part of my life. This secret only came to light at the birthday celebrations for my youngest son. Towards the end of the party a friend enquired if my son's Christian name had a family origin and I was taken aback when my husband declared: *"No, the birthday boy is named after Colin Harvey, the greatest midfield player of all time."* The news was a revelation and prompted me to recount that he had been very keen to take charge of the registration of the birth some 18 years earlier. I've always liked the name 'Colin' and have always admired Colin Harvey's commitment to Everton. When I think of the great team that we followed when we were courting, I suppose I should be relieved that our youngest wasn't named Colin Alan Brian Gordon Howard James John Joseph Sandy Thomas Downey.

George Orr: Harvey saved his best goals for special occasions and scored the second against West Brom to clinch the title. His cracker from outside of the box flew into the top corner of the Park End net. The whole ground erupted at the final-whistle and, like many of the 58,000 blueboys, I climbed onto the pitch and extracted a piece of turf as a souvenir. I'd planned to transplant it into our back-garden and showed my trophy to my dad. He was far from impressed: *"Looks to me like one soft sod has dug up another soft sod!"*

Sandy Brown: It was one of the first European ties to be decided on penalties and the drama started when Joe Royle took the first kick into the Gwladys Street goal. He launched a cannonball straight down the middle but unfortunately Wolfgang Kleff, the German keeper, never moved and the ball rebounded off him. To make matters worse, Klaus Sieloff sent Andy Rankin the wrong way to put Borussia Monchengladbach 0-1 up. Bally, our penalty king, found the bottom right-hand corner with ease before Herbert Laumen missed the target to make it 1-1. Then Johnny Morrissey, Josef Heynckes, Howard Kendall and Horst Koppel converted to keep the outcome finely-balanced. I'd replaced Keith Newton during the match and was next in line. I was a good striker of the ball and managed to fire my penalty kick towards the centre of the goal just as the keeper moved to his right. This meant that Ludwig Muller had to convert his effort to keep them in the competition. We all watched the climax from the centre-circle and, through the gaps in my fingers, I remember Andy flinging himself to his right and getting both hands to the ball. I think it was the only time that I've ever kissed a goalkeeper.

Francis Kane: I realise now that I loved Colin Harvey because he was what the School of Science was meant to be about - the craft, the mystery, and the magic. I was 14, my dad had just died and I really needed a hero. Death and its awful, mundane realities had mucked me about badly, so I probably endowed Harvey with even more heroic qualities although honestly, he did always appear to be seeing a greater, more majestic game in his mind than was being played out on the park. Thinking about this, decades later, I realise that he established a style template in my head, which would always determine whether I liked a player or not. The blue bloodline that ran through Duncan McKenzie, Tricky Trev, Pat Nevin and a few other greats will always be traced back to 'The White Pele'.

Dave Tickner: I don't remember them as individuals, rather as a unique midfield unit. Kendall, Harvey & Ball played as one with each member knowing instinctively where the other two were.

Ed Loftus: I was brought up in Burnand Street, a couple of doors from Archie Styles and about 150 yards from Anfield. On the Sunday before Howard and Archie left for Birmingham, I was coming back home from playing in Stanley Park. My mum was waiting on the step and demanded to know where I'd been because I'd just missed those two Evertonians playing footy in the street. I was absolutely mortified. If I'd have been there I don't know if I'd have asked them if I could join in, but just to have caught a glimpse of my heroes juggling the ball around outside our front door would have been enough.

Gordon Lee: Kendall, Harvey & Ball were an impossible act to follow. They had tremendous talent, an overwhelming will to win and worked hard too. They didn't really need to work so hard, but they did and that was why they were so great. If I was a manager and had them in my side today, I would fancy my chances against anyone including Manchester United.

Ed Stewart: Everton were walloped 0-6 at Chelsea and I decided to support them, more out of pity than anything else. I began to watch them in the sixties around the time of 'The Holy Trinity'. Kendall, Harvey & Ball were the best in the country. To watch them play was spell-binding because they had everything. They didn't get the credit they deserved because other clubs were deemed more fashionable. In fact, the whole team was short of recognition.

Dave Kelly: Thinking back about Colin Harvey, so many things spring to my mind - reading about his cool debut at the San Siro - defending him from over-critical fans who seemed to enjoy picking on the local lads - seeing him in a sharp Italian suit in Bootle on the morning of Tommy Wright's wedding - starting a Colin Harvey chant to the tune of 'Poison Ivy' after his 25-yarder found the net in a cup replay at Hillsborough - cheering his half-hit winner in the Burnden semi-final - drinking in the Warbreck pub one night with a couple of red-nosed mates when he walked in and I fell to my knees and bowed - being an important third of 'The Holy Trinity' - celebrating his England cap against Malta - marvelling at his fantastic strike against West Brom that sealed the championship - getting drunk the day he left Goodison. That's Colin Harvey - my all-time hero. The loyalty of the man to the royal blue cause is absolutely amazing.

Alex Wilson: 'The Holy Trinity' were a rarity in the British game, in that they were respected for the brilliance of their football. They combined the traditional values of toil and endeavour with technique and style. Perhaps Alf Ramsey's preference for sweat above skill kept Harvey and Kendall on the fringes of the England set-up - luxuries to be used against less demanding foes.

Brian Hall: Howard Kendall was a huge local star when I was going to the school near Deepdale. I was playing for Lancashire Grammar Schools and when I'd go round to my girlfriend's, her father liked to talk to me about football. One day her sister walked in with a new boyfriend, Howard Kendall, and her old man never really spoke to me again.

Mark Tallentire: My prized possession was a round-neck Everton shirt on the back of which my mum had sewn a white No 8 in honour of my first hero - Alan Ball. After I'd passed my eleven-plus, I immediately invested £4.75 on a pair of white boots from Jack Sharp's in Whitechapel. I remember not taking them off my feet for the first 48 hours. I wore them in the street, in the house and in bed. I also wore them when representing my school at rugby league during the half-time interval of the Widnes-Swinton game. After we'd finished the word spread that my hero was in the stands and my friend and I waited patiently at the exit until Alan Ball left his seat. We politely approached him: *"Please Mr Ball can I have your autograph?"* He dismissed us: *"Later fans. Later."* I took him at his word and followed him to a side-street near Naughton Park. His driver opened the door for him and before it closed I begged: *"Please sir, can I have your autograph?"* At that point my hero simply shook his head. Then his red Ford Capri spun away. The next day I bought a white No 7 from Gordon Harrison's sports shop in Widnes and my mum attached it to my blue shirt in honour of my hero - Alan Whittle.

Jim Emery: Sadly, we'll never see anything like 'The Holy Trinity' again. Nowadays the latest technology can capture every angle of the game and, as a consequence, supporters are more educated. Regrettably there wasn't much televised football in the late-1960s, so only old Evertonians have the privilege of recalling the rare qualities that Kendall, Harvey & Ball displayed. The rest of the world missed seeing three masters of the beautiful game.

A reign too fleeting ...

In the wake of two major set-backs in 1971, the pendulum of Merseyside football favoured Anfield.

Harry Ross: The team simply disintegrated. Ball was burned out, Harvey was injured, West lost form, and Labone and Morrissey were approaching retirement. The Lord never gets tired of testing Evertonians and we struggle to find meaning and value in a tragically flawed world!

Len Capeling: Everton had never made any great inroads into Europe and had stumbled into minefields in Dunfermline, Ujpesti Dozsa and Real Zaragoza. The poor showings against a modest Greek side were very disappointing, but no great surprise. It signalled the end.

Steve Kaiser: At one point we appeared destined to be the third British team to lift the trophy. But inexplicably we lost to an unknown side. That contest should have been decided at Goodison where shot after shot whistled around the Greek goal. Johnson, Wright and Ball all hit the woodwork and corner followed corner but to no avail. Had the ball run a little kinder, we could have taken a healthy lead to Athens. Our eventual defeat on the away goals rule was in its way a triumph for the tactical organisation of Ferenc Puskas, the manager of Panathinaikos. We have a unique record in the European Cup - during the past 35 years we've qualified to take part on four occasions but have lost only one game- way back in 1963.

John Keith: So much had been expected from Kendall, Harvey & Ball and the other Everton youngsters. After capturing the championship, they were fancied to do well in the European Cup and the FA Cup. After the disappointments of Athens, the Old Trafford defeat turned out to be the true watershed. Had Everton won, I believe that they would have triumphed over Arsenal in the final. But the gods of football didn't favour them that day. Harry Catterick's absence through illness proved to be a psychological advantage to Bill Shankly, who on learning of his rivals absence said: *"For a game like this, I'd have come in my coffin."* Shanks and Liverpool overcame an early goal from Alan Ball to take Everton's place at Wembley.

Phillip McNulty: I came home from school to discover that we'd been eliminated on the away goals rule - a concept alien to a 10-year old. Three days later I went to Old Trafford where we dominated the semi-final until Labone was injured. His loss resulted in massive gaps in our defence which Liverpool exploited. The royal blue magic was tarnished that day, but I think that the football gods were already favouring the Reds. The real turning point had been the 1970 derby at Anfield when we blew a 2-0 lead to go down 2-3. The record books show that Kendall, Harvey & Ball played only nine games together after the Old Trafford heart-break. Of those Everton won only two games - but one of them was against the Reds.

Wally Fielding: The Everton trio were as dominant in their heyday as Blanchflower, MacKay and White, the Tottenham stars who won the double in the early-sixties. They were tidy players with very sharp football brains and, for a little over two seasons, ran their opponents ragged. No-one could live with them yet they failed to take care of business against an inferior Greek team. Their subsequent demise can only be put down to Harry Catterick. I don't think that he'd changed from his playing days when he was a very hard man who would tread on his mother to get what he wanted. I also don't think that the club fully recovered from his illness.

Stan Bentham: I was a great admirer of Alan Ball, Howard Kendall and Colin Harvey. Like Cliff Britton and Joe Mercer, they were the best of their own era and a credit to our great club. Ironically, they also failed to realise their full potential. The ambitions of Mercer and my fellow team-mates were ruined by Adolf Hitler but I'm not sure who was responsible for the undoing of 'The Holy Trinity'.

Bobby Collins: They were grand players, especially Howard Kendall who is one of football's gentlemen. Colin was a competent boat-cleaner as a teenager and matured into an even better footballer. Great players like Kendall, Harvey & Ball are never happy with their performances, they're the ones who would come back for extra training. But Catterick's young team was just one of the many who have been tipped to conquer the world but never did.

Mike Pender: Alan Ball, Howard Kendall and Colin Harvey - in my own personal order of merit - were, without doubt, the most formidable midfield trio of their time. It's sad to say that had they been playing today, it wouldn't be in the royal blue of Everton. I say that for a number of reasons but realistically Everton could not afford them.

David Cairns: Why didn't we dominate Europe? I believe that 'The Catt' and his coaching ideas weren't up to it, though the players may well have been - sound familiar? Everton were amongst the last to embrace the four-man midfield. In truth, Panathinaikos did us for tactics - and came close to doing the whole of Europe too.

Mike Hughes: Towards the end of his days Alan Ball had become increasingly frustrated with the slide into mediocrity and had clashed with his team-mates on more than one occasion. I recall that one ugly confrontation with Howard Kendall turned into a Gough-Hutchison type of spat. It was embarrassing for all concerned, especially the Goodison faithful, because the grace, élan and style of Kendall, Harvey & Ball had done so much to restore the reputation of the School of Science. Their best performances were in 1968 when they conjured up so many great games, but if I was on death row in Texas and was granted the wish to watch one final Everton video it would have to be the Easter Saturday master-piece when we tore Chelsea to shreds. Kendall, Harvey & Ball were simply majestic and Everton banged three goals into the Park End in the opening minutes. We made it five, before declaring on the hour.

Jim Emery: Only once in a life-time can a club hope to unearth a player with the ability of an Alan Ball, a Colin Harvey or a Howard Kendall. I doubt if any club in the history of the English game had previously enjoyed the good fortune of discovering three players with such a wealth of abilities. So for one club to field Kendall, Harvey & Ball in the same team was simply a blessing from above. They were the ultimate in midfield harmony and played a naturally instinctive game. Of course, I realise that everything had to come to an end at some point - no matter how special it was. Evertonians cling jealously to their memories. What else is there? Kendall, Harvey & Ball R.I.P.

John McAllister: It wasn't easy following their exploits from the other side of the Irish Sea. The television reception was so bad that as a child I thought that Goodison Park was plagued by snow-storms. But there were no royal blue snowmen in those days and no-one disappeared when the midfield battles heated up. Kendall, Harvey & Ball also boasted immaculate ball skills in keeping with the traditions of the club but never indulged in over-elaboration. Their elegant foot-work was simply a bonus to their incredible efficiency, industry and consistency. 'The Holy Trinity' was a finely-tuned, turbo-charged machine which came without an extended warranty or readily-available spare parts. I remember the mystery related to Colin Harvey's injuries and the knee-jerk outrage to the transfer of Alan Ball but, with 20/20 hindsight, the candles had been blown out on the Goodison party cake by then.

Glyn Tudor: The gravitational spiral coincided with the introduction of a right pair of Newtons. As footballers - they flattered to deceive, as Evertonians - they were imposters. Keith was a classy defender for England but was no better than Sandy Brown at left-back. Henry was a very expensive enigma. An irrefutable fact is that during the two full seasons that they were at Goodison, we won only one game with both of them in the team.

Graham Wilson: Catterick's illness had a lot to do with the decline. With the taskmaster convalescing, life for some of our players was more enjoyable and possibly after reaching the Everest of the Division 1 title many had forgotten their reason for climbing it. Some appeared to be resting on their laurels. We let in too many goals, particularly on the road where we didn't win a League game for over a year. For the first time in a decade our defence was unsettled with frequent line-up changes at goalkeeper, left-back and centre-half. Labone's immense influence at the heart of the defence and on the team was sorely missed.

Ken Rogers: Ball and company reigned supreme and should have dominated English football for another five years. That the championship team broke up without capturing another major prize remains one of the great mysteries of modern football.

Len Capeling: In many ways Kendall's reign in the Goodison hot-seat mirrored that of Harry Catterick. Both won two Division 1 titles. Both created outstanding teams around phenomenal midfield units and both failed to establish dynasties. Catterick's 69/70 team fell apart after the sale of Ball and the loss of other stars such as Labone and Morrissey. Kendall's team fell apart after injuries to Reid and Bracewell and the defection of Trevor Steven.

Denis O'Meara: Our championship team was somewhat fragile, a situation exacerbated by the debilitating 1970 World Cup from which our England quartet came back more than a little jaded. The club was also negligent in not strengthening key positions. With the change in Alan Ball's role, we lacked a consistent goal-poacher to feed off Joe Royle. Husband and Whittle both lacked the necessary consistency to be true international class. The dilemma became more apparent during Ball's final season when his was restricted to only two goals. The defence also needed bolstering. Possibly Catterick was slow in buying a permanent replacement for Ray Wilson and the goalkeeping rivalry between West and Rankin, and then 'Dai the Drop' was unsettling. Prior to the horrendous 70/71 season, we'd always been one of the top four teams in the land. When Tommy Casey was given temporary charge of the poisoned chalice it was hardly surprising that the team imploded but the impact on the manager's health remains unknown.

George Orr: The rapid decline had much to do with Catterick's ill health. I don't know why the club didn't appoint an assistant to share the manager's burden. Also, it's hard to believe that we would sell Alan Ball without having a world-class replacement in mind, but none appeared. Although there was no shortage of new faces, the quality of his purchases was disappointing. Mike Bernard and 'Tiger' McLaughlin were never going to make much of an impression and Alan Whittle and Henry Newton were never allowed to reach their full potential.

Dave Prentice: Anfield trembled at the mere mention of their names. The pendulum only began to swing towards Anfield after the defection of Alan Ball but most Reds have been brainwashed into believing that they'd ruled Merseyside football since the arrival of Bill Shankly. This is an urban myth, because the Blues were the dominant side throughout the sixties accumulating 527 Division 1 points compared to Liverpool's 430. We were champions twice and only finished outside the top six in 1966 when we won the FA Cup.

Keith Newton: We were awash with team-spirit and had our own ideas about how the game should be played. Our championship line-up included several individuals who were very eager to learn about the game as well as the business of football. Four of them went on to manage clubs in the Premier League. Bally had a mercurial personality, perhaps not ideally suited for management. If we'd lost, he would be inconsolable and would disappear into a mood of black despair. But if we had triumphed he would sing in the bath with unbounded enthusiasm for at least half an hour. Love him or loathe him, it was impossible not to be affected by him.

Brian Harris: Harry started to put together his new team during my twilight years and, as a result, I only caught a glimpse of the sparkling stars of 'The Holy Trinity' from afar. I'd played for two seasons alongside Colin Harvey, who was a terrific youngster destined for the top, and had a handful of games with Alan Ball shortly after he'd arrived. They were both superb athletes who loved to run the legs off the older players in training. Alan bubbled with enthusiasm and could be a bit cocky at times, which no doubt had something to do with the fact that he'd already won a World Cup winners' medal. But I've never found his type of self-belief to be offensive, unlike Tony Kay who was an arrogant man. Alan was an immediate hit with all of his team-mates and all of the fans at Goodison. Players usually take a couple of games to weigh up new arrivals, but Alan was a revelation on his debut and seemed to get better with every game.

John Quinn: The disintegration of 'The Holy Trinity' started at Elland Road minutes after Joe Royle scored 'The Goal of the Decade' according to the papers. We lost 2-3.

Mark Tallentire: It was Duncan McKenzie's home debut in 1976 and the visitors' coach was parked on Goodison Road. As the Birmingham City team made their way to the main entrance, I spotted a balding figure in their ranks who established an immediate rapport with the fans. It was Howard Kendall but he seemed to have aged 10 years since he'd left the club three seasons earlier. Life without his beloved Everton must have been hard.

Ian MacDonald: Even kids from out of town could name our team - a tribute which is reserved for the best. I remember the final home game of the season when the West Brom players formed a guard of honour and applauded our heroes onto the pitch. We won 2-0 and I turned to my dad next to me in the Upper Bullens stand, hugged him and thanked him for bringing me into this world an Evertonian. Shortly afterwards, many of our key players were required for World Cup duty. Although Gordon West decided to stay in Maghull, Ball, Labone, Wright and Newton went to burn their lungs out at the high altitude of Mexico. Sadly these lads struggled to recapture their form during the following season, Harry Catterick was taken ill and then came a catastrophe which measured 10.0 on the Richter scale - Alan Ball was sold to Arsenal.

Mike Coville: Kendall, Harvey & Ball worked very hard for the team and it was a crying shame that they never appeared in the same England side together. We failed to conquer Europe because the club sat back on it's laurels. The manager sold Keith Newton and David Johnson and added Belfitt from Ipswich, Davies from Swansea and McLaughlin from Falkirk. None of whom are likely to be candidates for Gwladys Street's Hall of Fame any time soon.

Fred Pickering: I enjoyed half a-dozen games in the same side as Alan Ball during his first season and was impressed by his determination to bring additional success to the club. Everyone was touched by his charismatic presence and I'd never seen anyone get up and down the pitch quite like he could, but my abiding memory is of the young superstar scoring twice in the opening minutes of his first Merseyside derby. From that day the Everton fans have loved him and, of course, the Kopites have hated him. Afterwards he told me that he could've joined any club in the land but, having won the World Cup as a 20-year old, believed that there was only one place for him - Goodison Park.

Mike Brough: The most impressive performance was the humbling of Leeds. Our midfield unit was magnificent and out-played Bremner and Giles, but Johnny Morrissey was the real star that day. His wing-play tortured Paul Reaney, the England full-back. As the game entered the final minutes, I recall that the Everton wide-boy had the audacity to wedge the ball against the corner-flag and mimic looking at his watch. Both Reaney and Billy Bremner were shadowing him but neither was brave enough to attempt a tackle from behind.

They've sold Alan Ball ...

The sale of Alan Ball rocked Goodison and Evertonians of all ages felt betrayed by the club.

Dave Hickson: Alan Ball may have left in body but not in spirit. He always wore his blue heart on his sleeve - with pride. His transfer brought back the nightmare loss of Joe Mercer after the war. We've a history of letting great midfielders leave the club. Mercer, Collins, Ball and more recently Reid - all of them were special and all of them left before they should have done.

Tommy Jones: It was no surprise. Some claimed that Ball was burned out, others that he'd outstayed his welcome. Either way after five seasons of illuminating Goodison Park, the genie went back to his bottle and the stately old ground was never the same. I know that he liked to seek advice from his father and possibly they were ready to move on to greener pastures. Arsenal, the reigning champions and FA Cup holders, was an attractive destination.

Billy Williams: I was so gutted at the departure of my one and only boyhood hero that my dad let me travel to the Arsenal-Everton match on New Year's Day 1972 on my own at the tender age of 13. It was Ball's home debut for the Gunners. The match ended 1-1, but that was irrelevant. I was at the front of the old Clock End and the memory of the tremendous reception he received from the thousands of travelling Evertonians has remained with me to this day.

Gary Pepper: My dad broke the news. I was nine and the shock transfer broke my royal blue heart. Strangely his departure didn't fully sink in until the visit of Arsenal to Goodison in April. Our hero appeared in red and we were devastated! Everton had been playing poorly in his absence and gates had fallen to 25,000, but another 20,000 fans showed up to pay homage on his return to the third Merseyside cathedral - his spiritual home.

Neville Smith: The Everton manager embraced the fans' appreciation of Alan Ball and his non-stop commitment - then betrayed them by selling him to Arsenal. He was gone before we had really got to know him. I'd watched Blackpool at Stamford Bridge in 1965 when a young Ball had totally dictated the pattern of the game and I was thrilled when he joined us in 1966. Five years later, I was sick and can still see the smiles of Bertie Mee and Alan Ball on the back of the *Evening Standard*. It wasn't the end of the world, after all I had shed tears when we sold Bobby Collins, but Ball's departure plunged the club into anonymity for the next decade. He'd been the most revered Everton player since the halcyon days of 'The Golden Vision'. We have a history of transferring top-class players before their sell-by dates. I suppose that all clubs have their mysteries but I don't know why we have some of the darkest. Maybe that's why they call us 'The Blues'.

John Collings: I read about it in the *Daily Express*. It was a gift from Santa that I could've done without. Ball proved to be irreplaceable and Everton went steadily down hill.

David Evans: It was the first time I realised that football had dark corners and smoke-filled rooms where nasty deals were hatched. For years Alan Ball had been Everton. It made no sense and there was just emptiness. I remember *The Echo* calling the next match the first game of the PBE - the Post Ball Era. It really was that serious and a vast emotional blur. What was going on? I lost faith in Catterick. I lost faith in the natural order of things. I lost faith.

Steve Jones: I was watching television when to my surprise my mum came on the screen. Tony Gubba, who was working for the local BBC, was interviewing her outside the Toffee Shop where she had been Christmas shopping. He asked: *" What do you think about Alan Ball being transferred to Arsenal?* My mum said: *"Oh no! My old fella will do his nut!"*

Mike Burke: A mate of mine tells the story that this was the day he realised his mother was not omnipotent. It was the first time he had pleaded with her to make it not so, but she was powerless. No more would it be heard: *"Who's the greatest of them all? Little curly Alan Ball. What's the thing that we like most? Sandy Brown and beans on toast."*

Brendan Connolly: I attended St Edward's College, just down the road from Bellefield, and a friend had heard a rumour that Alan Ball was up for sale. It was a bombshell because every square inch of my bedroom wall had been covered with pictures of my hero - that is until I removed all traces of him. I remember staring at the holes left by the drawing pins for days, as I entered a period of mourning. He may have had red hair and white boots, but I had few doubts that he also had royal blue blood pumping through his veins.

Brian Tottey: The headlines of *The Echo* said it all: *"Everton star is Arsenal bound."* To make matters worse the front page included a photograph of Ball and his father smiling after meeting Bertie Mee. I was old enough to know that players come and go and wasn't really too bothered by him moving on to Highbury. Of course he was a national treasure but I'm not sure how much he loved the club during his playing days. I was more upset by the loss of Joe Royle, four years later almost to the day. Joe always put the best interests of the club first and was only 25 when he moved to Maine Road. We were left with Jim Pearson and Mike Lyons fighting over the No 9 shirt to partner Bob Latchford.

John O'Brien: It was like a family bereavement. There had always been something distinctly religious - something spiritual about him. Maybe it had to do with him being routinely included in our prayers. Certainly he'd been the answer to them. We had a miserable Christmas and mourned the loss of our flame-haired idol for months.

Phillip McNulty: As a 10-year old, I went to every home game. I didn't believe my dad when he told me that my hero was going down South. It took me weeks to recover - it took the club 13 years. Of course I was too young to appreciate the economics of football, but I was old enough to understand that no team flourished by selling its best player. I couldn't image him wearing colours other than the royal blue of the club that he loved.

Norman Dainty: I'd heard rumours about money problems but never saw the need for the club to transfer him. The championship team broke up after Ball went and the situation deteriorated further after Catterick stepped to one side. His replacements consigned us to mediocrity for a decade. Billy Bingham's sales of Kendall and Harvey had as much impact as the loss of Ball.

Ed Stewart: I heard the news at a party in London surrounded by people who didn't know anything about football. I withdrew to grieve in the corner all on my own but they kept on coming over to ask me what was wrong. All I could utter was: *"They've sold Alan Ball. They've sold Alan Ball."* Nobody could get me out of the doldrums no matter how hard they tried. I'm sure I ruined the party for everyone.

Rob Sharratt: There was one line in the *Sydney Morning Herald*. It just said: *"Alan Ball has joined Arsenal from Everton."* I couldn't find out anything else from anyone. Why would they do such a thing? Weren't we the millionaire club? It was bad enough when Alex Young left without my permission, but at least he was at the end of his career. Alan Ball was at his peak.

Phil Bowker: I can recall my dad walking round the house speaking in a squeaky voice: *"My name is Alan Ball and I'm off to The Arsenal."* I also remember that it wasn't funny. I'd already grown out of my favourite royal blue kit, with it's white cuffs and homemade No 8, but it was still a tough lesson to learn. I just couldn't understand why.

Keith Wilson: It was a cold December night, one of the darkest nights in my life. I was playing at the bottom of the stairs when my dad came home from work. He took the newspaper from the side pocket of his boiler-suit and gloated: *"Well that's the last you'll see of your idol."* The back-page confirmed my fears - Harry Catterick had sold Alan Ball. At the time I was far too young to understand why. I just knew that I would never see him in an Everton shirt again. My grandad, who had adored William Ralph Dean, and my dad, who had idolised Eddie Wainwright, tried to console me but I cried for days. I'd been told that the treatment Catterick had received at Blackpool, after he'd dropped Alex Young, had been out-of-order. But selling my Alan Ball - my idol - that was worthy of a public hanging at the Pier Head. As I grew older I realised that Everton Football Club is not about one player, no matter how good he may be.

Norman Houncell: Bally didn't live too far away from the Stork Hotel in Billinge and called in after his debut for Arsenal, a 1-1 draw at Forest. I was chatting with Tommy Wright and Jimmy Husband's mate Roy Wood of Wizzard. Bally wasn't interested in the bearded pop-star or his enormous afghan. He had tears in his eyes: *"Why have they got rid of me?"*

Jim King: The BBC broke the news to me in a cold and formal manner. But to this day I've never understood why he would want to desert his loyal flock. We all expected that the reasons would come out in the wash - but they never have. Of course, Merseyside was rife with ugly rumours and possibly the smoke screen has been maintained to protect the club.

Len Capeling: Ball had become the heartbeat of the club and his transfer was mind-boggling. I couldn't understand why the club let him go. There was lots of gossip but in those days the papers weren't too keen to investigate. As a result many unfounded stories have propagated. Not long afterwards Whittle and Johnson departed under similarly mysterious clouds.

Peter Stuart: The 69/70 campaign was tremendous. It was my first season of going to the game with my dad and I'd got a pair of white boots that Christmas. I can clearly remember Alan Ball leaving. I was devastated by the news and threw my boots into the bin. However, I've still got a nice photograph of me age six modelling them in my mother's back-garden.

Eddie Cavanagh: We've all heard the urban myths about certain blue boys which have circulated through the city's ale houses over the past few decades. The bile about excessive gambling, binge-drinking and the like has no foundation but has damaged the reputations of some outstanding Evertonians as well as that of a great football club.

Ed Loftus: My wife woke me up to break the news that Nick Barmby had taken the 30 pieces of silver and was off to Liverpool. Half a life-time on and now married with three kids of my own, it was the same feeling I'd had when my mum told me that Alan Ball had joined Arsenal. I couldn't speak and went to my room. She was so worried that she kept coming upstairs to see if I was all right. I put on a brave face and shrugged it off. But when she'd gone back downstairs, I cried. My tears were for Everton, for Alan and for me.

Mike Walls: My godmother told me we'd sold Alan Ball and I was really annoyed with her for days afterwards. It had all fallen apart already but nobody seems to know why. I don't think the team deteriorated at all after Ball's departure. We were already a poor side.

John McCormick: I was saddened by the departure of Colin Harvey to Sheffield but by then I'd been hardened by the character-building exercise of having to accept the betrayal of my hero. My dad said: *"No player is bigger than the club, not even Alan Ball."* For the first time, I questioned my old fella's judgement.

Colm Kavanagh: My main memory of the day is of my father refusing to put a pump on my bicycle. He'd been promising me for days and most of the other kids on the road already had theirs. I was a little too young to truly appreciate the horror of Ball's sale, but simply recall my dad being livid with the management, the board and anyone else he could point a finger at. I've a clearer picture of his reaction the day Howard was allowed to move to Birmingham. It put his angst at Ball's departure into the shade. To sell Alan Ball was a terrible error, to follow suit with Howard Kendall - well, words were not needed to accentuate his despair. I simply thanked the Lord that I already had my bicycle pump and shiny bell in place.

Steve Dingsdale: I'd thought that Alan Ball was an Evertonian through and through and couldn't believe that he would agree to leave us, even though his new club had just won the double. The manager in those days had a reputation for being economical with the facts. I recall that he said something like: *"I received an offer from Arsenal for Alan Ball. It was such a figure that it had to be placed before the board of directors immediately."* It was an untidy exit with too many questions left unanswered.

Colin Watt: Why on earth would an ambitious club sell its best player? I've researched the archives of the local newspapers to see how the press reacted. Michael Charters at *The Echo* wrote: *"Ball has pushed his slight frame beyond the limits of his physical capacity. He has given 100% so often that now he cannot give 100% although his heart wants to. I doubt if he now has the strength to sustain his play at the level of performance which made him, only 18 months ago, the greatest midfield player in British football."* But if Ball was burned out why were Arsenal prepared to break the British transfer record to recruit him?

Jon Berman: I was 13 playing 'blow football' at a friend's house. The transistor radio was on and all of a sudden the BBC proclaimed: *"England international Alan Ball has been sold to Arsenal for a record fee of £220,000."* The announcement was followed by interviews with Bertie Mee. My friend's mum tried to ply me with cakes but nothing could stop me crying. Ball was my hero - I had the white boots and all. When he left my whole world crashed around me. I thought that it was the end of Everton and that we'd never recover from it.

Denis O'Meara: Our Michael had a mop of red hair and was the spitting image of Alan Ball. Like many of the 10-year olds in Kirkby, he owned a pair of white boots and would wear them everywhere - even in the house. He felt betrayed by the news of the sale and I can vividly remember him running home from St Joseph's school crying: *"Tell me it's not true."*

George Orr: Ball was our very own Dick Whittington who went to London to seek his fortune. I first read about his sensational transfer in the *Daily Mirror*. It stunned Evertonians everywhere and we couldn't accept that he'd want to leave us or that we would ever contemplate selling him. Not all of his contributions were positive towards the end but even so the deal never made sense. We had taken great pride in being called 'The Bank of England Club' and I can't believe that we needed the cash for new players. I can recall that the chairman, George Watts, expressed his confidence in the manager's handling of the deal and reassured us that funds were available for the right players but that we were not going to spend money on signings no better than the players already on the books. Harry Catterick had a reputation for moving quickly in the transfer market and for buying quality, that is until he sought a replacement for Ball. Maybe our expectations were unrealistic because within months he had squandered his nest-egg on the likes of Lawson, Bernard and, of course, Bernie Wright. The subsequent decline led to Bingham's virtuosi playing second fiddle in the Merseyside symphony.

Mike Owen: It was my first moment of intense blue anger and dismay, and far more traumatic than being told Father Christmas didn't exist, but then perhaps that was because he wore red.

Ged Creighton: I arrived home from secondary school. My mother looked sad: "*Should I tell him or will you?*" My dad had tears in his eyes as he gasped: "*Alan Ball's going to Arsenal, pending a medical.*" I cried my eyes out as I went to my room. I prayed for him to fail his medical. The six o'clock news caused me to question my faith.

George Stuart: One of my mates told me at the school bus stop, but I didn't believe him. Then the bus conductor confirmed my deepest fears: "*Yup! Just been on the radio. Sold to Arsenal for £200,000.*" My best mate was a Red and was really hard as far as footie was concerned. He just looked at me and laughed. But he soon stopped. I guess he had never seen me cry since primary school. I'm holding back the tears now, for what might have been.

Chris Gill: It was an unremarkable cold December morning. I'd just passed my seventeenth birthday and the last drops of finally diminishing euphoria from our championship triumph carried me to work. As usual I'd scraped my shoes scaling the back-wall and, en-route to Kirkby station, nipped into the local shop for the *Daily Mirror*. It was there that my world was turned upside down. "*Arsenal sign Alan Ball*" roared the front-page, offensively. Usually, I didn't get to the front of the paper until last, if at all. Stunned, I felt incredulity and disbelief followed by a rising tide of anger as I pored incessantly and almost tearfully over the same hideous words. It was a knife through the heart, a betrayal of a love affair. The man with the white boots had gone and football life was never going to be the same. Even now I can still feel the pain.

Ronnie Jones: I was gutted by his transfer on 22-12-1971. I honestly don't remember where I was when JFK was shot but I learned about the loss of Alan Ball from *The Echo*. I still have the cuttings: "*Ball who says goodbye to his colleagues today after a morning training session will meet them as opponents at Highbury on New Year's Day. Ball's statutory entitlement from the deal is about £11,000, but the financial arrangements are such that he is probably the richest player in British football at the present time. Alan Ball Senior, manager of Preston North End, said: This is a fabulous deal for Alan. Neither he nor anyone else could have refused it. It goes a long way towards securing his future and I should be surprised if there is a better paid player in Britain. The terms are that good.*" The whole episode caused trauma amongst Everton supporters and provided an illuminating glimpse into the business of football.

Billy Williams: My favourite memory of Alan Ball is him waving to me and my dad when taking a corner at Derby in December 1971. Of course he won't remember, but I've never forgotten because it was his last game in a royal blue shirt. We lost 0-2.

Ronnie Goodlass: I'd been at the club a couple of years by then and was walking up to Bellefield. Hundreds of fans were waiting in Sandforth Road. One of them stopped me on the pavement and asked: "*Ronnie, is it true?*" I didn't know anything but as I walked through the gates, I soon realised that it must be true because it felt as if somebody had died. They had, he was Mr Everton. When I look at the present day game nothing surprises me, but back then it was the biggest shock in football. One minute he was here and the next he was gone, it was as if you were in a dream wanting to wake up hoping that it wouldn't be true.

John McFarlane: As a postman, I'd catch the 4.00 am radio news. This one cold December morning I was startled by the announcement: "*Alan Ball, the 26-year old England ace, has joined Arsenal for a British record transfer fee.*" It was a bolt out of the blue and I remember trudging around the streets of Skelmersdale trying to come to terms with the loss of one of the all-time Everton greats. I tried to temper my despair with thoughts of his faults. For example, he lacked the diplomatic skills expected of an Everton captain and I recalled the way he'd tore into Keith Newton, his fellow international, in front of 40,000 on-lookers at Leeds.

Barry Hewitt: I was the only kid in the Ipswich Sunday League wearing size 10 white boots. I'd ordered my Hummel specials from Mick McNeil's sports-outfitters and they immediately added an edge to my game - as a goalie. Alan Ball was my boyhood hero and, with his name in the programme line-up, I was confident that we could beat anyone, anywhere. I was shocked by his move to Highbury and refused to believe that he would even contemplate leaving the club. At the time I reckoned it was a conspiracy and that he'd been pushed out. Possibly I overlooked the facts that he'd gone through a lean spell, by his standards, and that his Midas touch had deserted him in front of goal. Then after a while I realised that he may have grown too big for his own white boots or perhaps too big for the manager to handle. Having said that, he still is the greatest player to have pulled on an Everton shirt in my life-time.

Joe Lloyden: Ball was a Blue, definitely not a fickle mercenary, but there was a sort of inevitability about it all. He'd been lost to us for 20 months, since he'd been appointed captain.

Charlie Hengler: Ball had been raised by his old fella to be a good pro and epitomised everything that was great about our magnificent team of the late-1960s. I was shaken by the news but wasn't surprised. The rumour mill had been working over-time with all sorts of scandalous allegations. There was only one Alan Ball and Harry Catterick never had a hope in hell of replacing him like-for-like. I was also gutted when Kendall moved to Birmingham in 1974 but on that occasion we got to feast on the goals of Bob Latchford for several seasons. When Ball moved to Arsenal, we were fed a staple diet of Mick Bernard.

Mike Royden: I prefer to remember the day when Ball signed for us. I was 10 and my dad came home early to tell me about it at the front-gate - its weird how I have such a clear memory of this. We could not believe such a major World Cup star had signed for us. Then my mate and I went around the streets in our blue shirts composing songs about him. Later we saw the publicity shots of him in his blue shirt for the first time - there was one of him at Bellefield with one knee on the grass and his hand resting on a football. We did that pose and took photos. When my dad died a couple of years ago I was clearing his desk and found the picture in his drawer. He didn't really leave me anything personal, so I took that.

John Quinn: My friend Paul, a sub-editor for *The Echo,* rang at about 3.00 pm: *"You've just gone and signed Latchford ..."* Everyone knew the qualities that Bob Latchford had and it seemed quite fitting that Everton, the richest club in the country, would continue its policy of attracting only the best and we had always specialised in magical centre-forwards. This was very good news. Then the rest of Paul's sentence registered in my mind "*... Kendall is going the other way in part exchange, but the details and the news won't be released until tomorrow."* Now this was very bad news indeed. I met a few friends later that night at the pub and gave them the scoop. They too were more concerned with the departure of Kendall than the arrival of Latchford. It was another major step into a decade of darkness.

Gerard Dignam I was angered by Ball going to Arsenal and by Kendall going to Birmingham, but was devastated by the loss of Harvey. He was one of us. The week after he moved to Sheffield Wednesday - it was in September 1974 - some true Blues draped a big banner over the balcony of the Park End stand proclaiming: *"Colin Harvey - The White Pele."* I think that it was targeted at Billy Bingham, the new manager, but maybe it was directed towards heaven.

Bryan Doran: Have we seen the last of Alan Ball MBE at Everton? He seems to prefer to exploit his nation-wide celebrity through the World Cup Winners' Sporting Club where, for £1,966 per year, fans can mingle with members of the triumphant England team at various sporting and social events. Despite the mystery associated with his defection, Ball will always be a son of Gwladys Street. Perhaps not a favourite son - more an illegitimate sprog.

David Cairns: My dad told me and I thought he was winding me up. Ball had scored the only goal in my first Everton match and was my hero of proportions to which no other sportsman could aspire. And as for Arsenal, they'd taken our title in 1971 and won the double - bonus points for their FA Cup win though! To me it was an absolute tragedy that they'd kidnapped my hero. Oddly enough it gave me a soft spot for Arsenal that remains to this day.

San Presland: I painstakingly used a ruler to measure points on the picture I was copying and scaled them up to mark out the points on my drawing. The effect was a giant dot-to-dot portrait of Alan Ball. Imagine my surprise a few days later when it had disappeared! Eventually my mum confessed that she'd sent it to Everton to get it signed by the great man himself. I was horrified and burst into tears. I know she'd meant well but the next few days were agony. Constantly, I visualised him getting this picture and bursting out laughing, then passing it round all the other players where they would likewise roll around hysterically. About one week later, it came back, not crumpled or abused but neatly rolled in a tube and there in large letters in the bottom right-hand corner: *"Best Wishes, Alan Ball."* And so it was that my only drawing ever to find itself framed and displayed to the world was really just an insignificant addendum to a most excellent autograph.

Derek Hatton: I walked into the pub near my university in London and someone told me that Arsenal had signed Alan Ball. I thought it was just a bad joke. After numerous phone calls I established that it was true and I couldn't think straight for days.

Mike Hughes: I'd collected hundreds of autographs from outside Bellefield during the school holidays and had found Alan Ball to be one of the more obliging stars. He was my hero, the first all-action midfielder who could score goals - a fore-runner of Paul Scholes, only five-times better. I'd got wind of his move to Arsenal as I walked back from Cardinal Allen School and my fears were confirmed shortly after I popped into the newsagents in Old Swan. I was horrified by the headlines and hoped that *The Echo* had made a mistake. When I got home I sought solace in the huge posters of him which adorned my bedroom walls. They remained in place for years, after all he was my hero and perhaps he might have returned home some day.

Bill Kenwright: I learned about the tragedy from the back-page of *The Evening Standard* and recall that the headlines had a pro-Arsenal bias. The mere thought of Alan Ball playing in red turned my stomach. Although he hadn't been at his best for a couple of months, I felt a deep sense of betrayal. After all, the directors had sold my three greatest heroes - Dave Hickson twice, Alex Young and now Alan Ball - and I was convinced that they didn't know what the hell they were doing. My grief was compounded by reflections of the pride that I'd felt when Ball signed for us shortly after the World Cup final. He had done as much as anyone to win the trophy for England and could've gone anywhere. Alan Ball chose Everton.

Mike Coville: I was at work in Bradford when the news hit me. My colleagues who were supporters of Leeds and Manchester United made sure I was aware of the fact that we had sold our ace. I tried to maintain a stiff upper-lip but I was devastated by the news.

Jim Emery: Nowadays people are more impervious to events but back then larger-than-life incidents took a while to register. For Evertonians, the loss of Alan Ball was one of those incidents when you do remember where you were, a bit like the death of JFK, John Lennon and Princess Diana. I remember staring at the radio in disbelief and feeling like it was the end of a dream. He'd become a corner-stone cemented in the Goodison establishment and the manager had no chance of finding another one like him. Ball was such a tremendous footballer - he had everything in a mixed grill including an enormous amount of fillet steak.

Sid McGuiness: I lived in Goodison Avenue and saw Bally on the pitch having his photograph taken by *The Daily Mirror*. When I crossed the sacred turf to say goodbye to him, I recall that he looked a little confused about his move to London. He shook me by the hand and we both had a little cry. Then he said: *"Sid, here's something for you to remember me by!"* It was his famous white boots. When I got them back home, I immediately stuffed the toes with an old pair of his England socks, soaked in Vaseline, which he had previously given to me. In those days he would only change his boots at the beginning of each season and I couldn't help but think that there must have been at least another 20 great games for Everton left in them. I believe that Bally always thought that he played better in his white boots. So much so that before one game, he was horrified to discover that he'd left them at Bellefield. With the kick-off approaching, I painted a pair of his training boots white. I even shaded in the trademark chevrons with a black marker. As luck would have it, the heavens opened. So at half-time I had to solicit the help of Phil Wang, the Goodison maintenance man, to give them a second coat.

Jackie Hamilton: I was enjoying a pint in the Eagle and Child pub when Eddie Cavanagh broke the news. We were sick because we knew that Alan Ball never wanted to leave us. I've had the pleasure of meeting him many times on the sportsmen's dinner circuit and believe that the whispers about his debts were absolute nonsense. He was told by Everton that he was no longer wanted but subsequently has been the victim of smear and innuendo.

Garry Doolan: Merseyside folklore dictates that Liverpool play in red so that their blood will merge with the colour of their shirts - and that Everton wear royal blue for the same reason. Legend also has it that the Kop laughed every time that Alan Ball pulled on the red of Arsenal.

Ian MacDonald: A man gibbering unintelligibly came into the pub and spat out that Alan Ball had been sold to Arsenal. Confirmation came from my dad and I cried. The jewel in the crown of our midfield was sold at a fiscal profit but at a terrible loss to the supporters who idolised him. An unholy board had desecrated 'The Holy Trinity'. Surely a talent like Ball should have been fought for and whatever problems that may have existed could have been overcome.

Fred Webb: Alan Ball loved putting Liverpool in their place and I've fond memories of the 1967 FA Cup tie. Tickets were really hard to come by but somehow my mate Ernie and I managed to obtain one for Gwladys Street and another for the old Park End, where the Reds liked to congregate. The demand had resulted in the game being screened at Anfield and had also oiled some of the local amateur printing presses. In fact, my Park End ticket looked more than a bit dodgy but I thought that since it was a night game I'd chance my luck at the turnstile. While I was plucking up my courage, a friendly Kopite approached me and asked if he could swap his Gwladys Street ticket for mine. The deal was done and I'd scrambled into the sanctuary of Goodison before the ink had dried on his red fingers. Of course, it was Alan Ball who had the last laugh. He never ever let Everton down.

Rick Fazackerley: He was the only modern superstar we'd had and when he came back to his old stomping ground with Southampton the whole stadium sang his name. I recall reading that he was so overwhelmed that he had difficulty getting going for the first 20 minutes.

Phil Parker: Alan Ball was my all-time hero and it was sad to witness his increasing frustrations towards the end of his Everton days. I remember the clash with West Ham immediately after the Old Trafford semi-final defeat. The mood at Goodison was sombre, the attendance was below 30,000 and Howard Kendall had put through his own goal, nevertheless I can vividly picture Ball venting his anger at being body-checked by Billy Bonds. He retaliated by putting his hands around the defender's throat. The sight of his team-mates trying to loosen his strangle-hold sent out a clear signal that the glory days were numbered.

Blind admiration ...

Fans of all ages, many too young to have seen them in action, adopt 'The Holy Trinity' as the benchmark for assessing modern midfielders.

Dave Prentice: Tales of their intricate passing are spine-tingling. Perhaps in my mind they are better than they were in reality. They certainly made life difficult for the next generation of midfield mortals such as Buckley, Clements and Dobson. Of course, the quartet of Steven, Reid, Bracewell and Sheedy was outstanding in the glory years but even they failed to lay to rest the ghosts of their illustrious predecessors. I doubt if we'll ever see the likes of them again.

Mark Denny: Although Reid and company collected more silverware, the Goodison measure for midfield power and finesse remains 'The Holy Trinity'. Why they failed to win more trophies remains a mystery, one of the many associated with our club. Everton has never kept the fans informed. The club sought no inputs before the construction of the Park End stand or the change in team colours to One 2 One blue. The lack of debate during the Johnson years over the move from our ancestral home was shameful. Goodison is the home of 'The Holy Trinity'.

Phil Redmond: I know them by their reputation for entertaining football. My dad loved to talk for hours about the sophisticated ball skills, intricate passing, tenacious tackling and incredible stamina of the flame-haired genius and his two lieutenants. 'The Holy Trinity' were a major part of my Goodison education. Obviously the game has changed since then and comparisons with players from other eras are unreliable. From my dad's accounts they overwhelmed opponents, possibly more so than Reid, Steven, Bracewell and Sheedy did 15 years later.

Mark Staniford: My dad told me that they were the soul of the team. Harvey and Kendall did the donkey-work like tackling, running and making space and Ball was the flair player. He still gets excited talking about Alan Ball - the greatest player of his generation. To hear people recount their tales of where they were when they heard that he'd been sold is a bit like asking: *"Where were you when Kennedy was assassinated."* In Ball's case, my dad was on a bus and overheard a conversation - he said it felt like a member of the family had died.

Peter Hackett: I was raised to believe that a gifted midfield was the platform for success and that an undistinguished one was a recipe for an end-of-season scrap. Kendall, Harvey & Ball should be studied by everyone who cares about the moribund condition of our great club.

Claire Gray: My first-hand experience of Kendall, Harvey & Ball has been limited to videos and stories. They were legends in their own time - I'd had that drummed into me from a very early age. A few months ago I was privileged to sit around a table with them, with not a single other person in the room. At that time their importance to Everton suddenly became very real. Recalling their past glories with such passion and clarity, for half an hour Howard Kendall, Colin Harvey and Alan Ball recreated a bit of Goodison history to the point that it felt like I'd been there myself. Their admiration for each other was obvious.

Martin O'Boyle: I was asked by the founder of Gwladys Street's Hall of Fame to help verify the lists of top-10 nominations submitted by 100 former-players. Ball's name appeared on every single ballot and he finished way ahead of post-war Goodison icons like Young, Labone, Wilson, Kendall, Harvey, Latchford and Reid. Many former-players couldn't resist adding a few words about his immense contributions to the club. Their plaudits included: *"the best player I've ever seen and the best I've ever played alongside ... a winner who shed blood, sweat and tears every time he pulled on the blue shirt ... he struck fear into the heart of the Kop every time he swaggered on to the Anfield turf ..."* and so on.

Paul Dwyer: I was brain-washed as a child. My dad loved the numbering of the Everton midfielders - No 4 Kendall - No 6 Harvey - No 8 Ball and would lean over my pram and ask me: *"Four, six, eight who do we appreciate? Ev-er-ton!"*

Graeme Sharp: Colin could play 'keep-up' with a tennis ball hundreds of times in a row and I shudder to imagine what he was like as a player. When I first came down from Scotland, he worked us hard. He'd say: *"If I didn't have faith in you, I wouldn't be wasting my time."* Colin had a short-fuse but his bullying made me a much better player. He could be a little shit in training and our 5-a-sides never finished until his side triumphed. There was never too many volunteers to be in his team and when he'd give the bibs out, I'd pray that he wouldn't pick me because he'd work my socks off. The losers would have to complete a 12-minute lap around Bellefield and those who finished behind him had to do another lap. Despite his troublesome hips, he'd sprint at the finish to make us work that bit harder.

Gary Stevens: Of all the people that I've met in football, Colin Harvey is the man that I respect the most. He spent endless hours working on my game at Bellefield and I can categorically state that if it hadn't been for him I wouldn't have enjoyed the successful career that I did.

Andy Hunter: I doubt if stars of their quality would want to play for the Everton of today. No doubt Goodison would still be the first choice of Colin Harvey. But their Premiership rivals wouldn't be keen on one team cornering the abundance of riches associated with Kendall, Harvey & Ball. But when you read the transfer fees for modern-day counterparts, any valuation of Alan Ball would approach £30 million. Ball made things happen, he was a world beater!

Derek Mountfield: I never had a pair of white boots as a child, I guess you had to be a bit flash to wear such footwear. However I did own a blue round-neck shirt with a No 4 sewn on the back. It was a present from my parents on my seventh birthday. Kendall, Harvey & Ball were the yardstick for the older generation to measure the prowess of midfielders and deserve their place in Everton folklore. Perhaps the only players to have reached that standard since then were Peter Reid, Paul Bracewell and the other lads from the mid-1980s.

Andy Gray: Howard was a wonderful man-manager and I thought that the Kendall-Harvey blend was ideal. Colin was more studious and very much a coach.

Chris Beesley: Of course I've only seen the videos of some of their matches, read about their accomplishments and noticed my grandfather and father salivate at the mere mention of their names. From all accounts Kendall, Harvey & Ball were a class act. Sadly, their commitment to stylish play seems to have eluded the Everton sides of my generation.

Alan Myers: Colin and Howard have enjoyed a productive friendship for over 30 years. They have an almost unspoken understanding, no doubt developed during their playing days as part of 'The Holy Trinity'. Their instinctive knowledge of what the other one wants helped to engineer a massive turn-around in the club's fortunes in the 1980s. I know when Howard came back the second time that Colin Harvey's name was at the top of his list of requirements.

Trevor Steven: Colin Harvey and Howard Kendall made a great team. Colin was driven by football to the point of crippling himself in training every day. His sessions were incredibly competitive - and he often left me stunned at his commitment.

Andy Clarke: I am a tad too young to remember them playing, but I do remember pulling an Alan Ball out of the Lucky Dip at a school fair. He was metal and about three inches high, it made by day! I kept him, even though he was wearing an Arsenal kit.

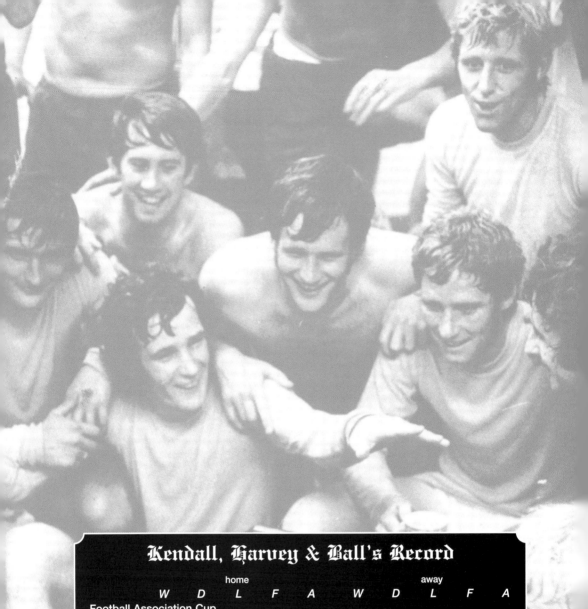

Kendall, Harvey & Ball's Record

	home					away				
	W	D	L	F	A	W	D	L	F	A
Football Association Cup										
1968	0	0	0	0	0	2	0	1	3	1
1969	1	0	0	2	1	0	0	1	0	1
1971	4	0	0	11	0	0	0	1	1	2
Total	**5**	**0**	**0**	**13**	**1**	**2**	**0**	**3**	**4**	**4**
Football League Cup										
1967/68	0	0	1	2	3	1	0	0	5	0
1968/69	2	1	0	9	1	0	0	1	0	1
1969/70	1	0	0	1	0	1	1	0	1	0
Total	**3**	**1**	**1**	**12**	**4**	**2**	**1**	**1**	**6**	**1**
European Cup										
1970/71	1	2	0	8	4	1	2	0	4	1
Football Association Charity Shield										
1970	0	0	0	0	0	1	0	0	2	1

Royal Blue Chronicles

reports of their domination

Everton v Manchester United 1967/68

West Bromwich Albion v Everton 1967/68

Everton v Leicester City 1968/69

Everton v Leeds United 1969/70

Liverpool v Everton 1969/70

Everton v Chelsea 1969/70

			Competition	Opposition	Result	Holy Trinity Goals	Attendance
1967	Mar 18	h	Division 1	Southampton	0-1		44,997
	Mar 22	h	Division 1	Tottenham Hotspur	0-1		50,108
	Mar 25	a	Division 1	Sunderland	2-0		34,134
	Apr 19	h	Division 1	Chelsea	3-1		39,316
	Aug 19	h	Division 1	Manchester United	3-1	Ball 2	61,452
	Aug 23	a	Division 1	Tottenham Hotspur	1-1		53,809
	Sep 2	h	Division 1	Wolverhampton Wanderers	4-2	Ball 2	51,498
	Sep 5	h	Division 1	West Ham United	2-0	Kendall	46,762
	Sep 9	a	Division 1	Fulham	1-2		25,366
	Sep 13	a	FL Cup	Bristol City	5-0	Kendall 2	22,054
	Sep 16	h	Division 1	Leeds United	0-1		53,179
	Sep 23	a	Division 1	Liverpool	0-1		54,189
	Sep 30	a	Division 1	Leicester City	2-0	Ball 2	22,768
	Oct 7	h	Division 1	Southampton	4-2	Ball, Kendall	47,896
	Oct 11	h	FL Cup	Sunderland	2-3		39,919
	Oct 24	h	Division 1	West Ham United	2-1	Kendall	44,092
	Oct 28	a	Division 1	Newcastle United	0-1		34,030
	Nov 4	h	Division 1	Manchester City	1-1		47,144
	Nov 18	h	Division 1	Sheffield United	1-0		37,994
	Nov 25	a	Division 1	Coventry City	2-0		32,330
	Dec 2	h	Division 1	Nottingham Forest	1-0		44,765
	Dec 9	a	Division 1	Stoke City	0-1		34,434
	Dec 16	a	Division 1	Manchester United	1-3		57,078
	Dec 23	h	Division 1	Sunderland	3-0	Ball	38,216
	Dec 26	h	Division 1	Burnley	2-0	Ball	54,324
1968	Jan 20	a	Division 1	Leeds United	0-2		44,119
	Jan 27	a	FA Cup	Southport	1-0		19,000
	Feb 3	h	Division 1	Liverpool	1-0	Kendall	64,482
	Feb 17	a	FA Cup	Carlisle United	2-0		25,000
	Feb 26	a	Division 1	Southampton	2-3	Ball	25,860
	Mar 2	h	Division 1	Coventry City	3-1	Ball	38,804
	Apr 13	a	Division 1	Sheffield United	1-0	Ball	25,547
	Apr 29	a	Division 1	Manchester City	0-2		37,786
	May 4	h	Division 1	Stoke City	3-0	Ball 2	43,302
	May 18	w	FA Cup	West Bromwich Albion	0-1		100,000
	Aug 10	a	Division 1	Manchester United	1-2	Ball	61,311
	Aug 13	h	Division 1	Burnley	3-0	Ball	48,903
	Aug 17	h	Division 1	Tottenham Hotspur	0-2		56,570
	Aug 19	a	Division 1	West Ham United	4-1	Ball, Harvey	34,895
	Aug 24	a	Division 1	Newcastle United	0-0		38,851
	Aug 27	h	Division 1	Liverpool	0-0		63,938
	Aug 31	h	Division 1	Nottingham Forest	2-1		45,951
	Sep 3	a	FL Cup	Tranmere Rovers	4-0	Ball	34,477
	Sep 7	a	Division 1	Chelsea	1-1		42,017
	Sep 14	h	Division 1	Sheffield Wednesday	3-0		44,517
	Sep 21	a	Division 1	Coventry City	2-2		37,846
	Sep 24	h	FL Cup	Luton Town	5-1	Ball	30,405
	Sep 28	h	Division 1	West Bromwich Albion	4-0	Ball 3, Harvey	47,792
	Oct 5	h	Division 1	Manchester City	2-0	Ball	55,399
	Oct 8	a	Division 1	Liverpool	1-1	Ball	54,496
	Oct 12	a	Division 1	Southampton	5-2	Ball	21,688
	Oct 16	h	FL Cup	Derby County	0-0		44,705
	Oct 19	h	Division 1	Stoke City	2-1	Harvey	42,887
	Oct 23	a	FL Cup	Derby County	0-1		34,370
	Oct 26	a	Division 1	Wolverhampton Wanderers	2-1	Ball	34,744
	Nov 2	h	Division 1	Sunderland	2-0	Ball	40,492
	Nov 9	a	Division 1	Ipswich Town	2-2		23,049
	Nov 23	a	Division 1	Leeds United	1-2		41,716
	Nov 30	h	Division 1	Leicester City	7-1	Ball	42,492
	Dec 7	a	Division 1	Arsenal	1-3	Ball	40,108
	Dec 21	a	Division 1	Stoke City	0-0		20,507
	Dec 26	a	Division 1	Manchester City	3-1		53,549
1969	Jan 4	h	FA Cup	Ipswich Town	2-1		49,047
	Mar 22	v	FA Cup	Manchester City	0-1		63,025
	Sep 3	a	FL Cup	Darlington	1-0	Ball	13,860
	Sep 6	a	Division 1	Derby County	1-2	Kendall	37,078
	Sep 13	h	Division 1	West Ham United	2-0	Ball	49,052
	Sep 17	a	Division 1	Newcastle United	2-1		37,094
	Sep 20	a	Division 1	Ipswich Town	3-0	Ball, Harvey	23,258
	Sep 24	a	FL Cup	Arsenal	0-0		36,119

o *Old Trafford*   v *Villa Park*   w *Wembley Stadium*

			Competition	Opposition	Result	Holy Trinity Goals	Attendance
1969	Sep 27	h	Division 1	Southampton	4-2		46,942
	Oct 1	h	FL Cup	Arsenal	1-0	Kendall	41,140
	Oct 4	a	Division 1	Wolverhampton Wanderers	3-2	Harvey	40,836
	Oct 8	a	Division 1	Crystal Palace	0-0		33,967
	Oct 11	h	Division 1	Sunderland	3-1	Kendall	47,271
	Oct 18	h	Division 1	Stoke City	6-2	Ball	48,663
	Oct 25	a	Division 1	Coventry City	1-0		37,816
	Nov 1	h	Division 1	Nottingham Forest	1-0		49,610
	Nov 8	a	Division 1	West Bromwich Albion	0-2		34,298
	Nov 15	a	Division 1	Chelsea	1-1		49,895
1970	Feb 21	h	Division 1	Coventry City	0-0		45,934
	Feb 28	a	Division 1	Nottingham Forest	1-1		29,174
	Mar 7	a	Division 1	Burnley	2-1	Ball	21,114
	Mar 11	a	Division 1	Tottenham Hotspur	1-0		27,764
	Mar 14	h	Division 1	Tottenham Hotspur	3-2	Ball	51,533
	Mar 21	a	Division 1	Liverpool	2-0		54,496
	Mar 28	h	Division 1	Chelsea	5-2	Ball, Kendall	58,337
	Mar 30	a	Division 1	Stoke City	1-0		33,111
	Apr 1	h	Division 1	West Bromwich Albion	2-0	Harvey	58,523
	Apr 4	a	Division 1	Sheffield Wednesday	1-0		30,690
	Apr 8	a	Division 1	Sunderland	0-0		28,774
	Aug 8	a	Charity Shield	Chelsea	2-1	Kendall	43,547
	Aug 15	h	Division 1	Arsenal	2-2		50,248
	Aug 18	h	Division 1	Burnley	1-1		44,717
	Aug 29	h	Division 1	Manchester City	0-1		50,724
	Sep 2	a	Division 1	Manchester United	0-2		49,599
	Sep 5	a	Division 1	West Ham United	2-1		29,171
	Sep 12	h	Division 1	Ipswich Town	2-0	Kendall	41,596
	Sep 16	h	European Cup	AB Keflavik	6-2	Ball 3	28,444
	Sep 19	a	Division 1	Blackpool	2-0		30,705
	Sep 26	h	Division 1	Crystal Palace	3-1	Harvey	43,443
	Sep 30	a	European Cup	AB Keflavik	3-0		9,500
	Oct 3	a	Division 1	Coventry City	1-3		29,212
	Oct 17	a	Division 1	Arsenal	0-4		50,053
	Oct 21	a	European Cup	Borussia Monchengladbach	1-1	Kendall	32,000
	Oct 24	h	Division 1	Newcastle United	3-1	Kendall	43,135
	Oct 31	a	Division 1	West Bromwich Albion	0-3		29,628
	Nov 4	h	European Cup	Borussia Monchengladbach	1-1		42,744
	Nov 7	h	Division 1	Nottingham Forest	1-0		39,255
	Nov 21	a	Division 1	Liverpool	2-3		53,777
	Nov 28	h	Division 1	Tottenham Hotspur	0-0		44,301
	Dec 5	a	Division 1	Huddersfield Town	1-1	Ball	27,658
	Dec 12	h	Division 1	Southampton	4-1		31,139
	Dec 19	h	Division 1	Leeds United	0-1		47,393
	Dec 26	a	Division 1	Wolverhampton Wanderers	0-2		30,178
1971	Jan 2	h	FA Cup	Blackburn Rovers	2-0		40,471
	Jan 9	a	Division 1	Burnley	2-2		17,512
	Jan 16	h	Division 1	Chelsea	3-0		43,628
	Jan 23	h	FA Cup	Middlesbrough	3-0	Harvey	54,557
	Jan 30	a	Division 1	Tottenham Hotspur	1-2		42,105
	Feb 6	h	Division 1	Huddersfield Town	2-1		37,213
	Feb 13	h	FA Cup	Derby County	1-0		53,490
	Feb 20	h	Division 1	Liverpool	0-0		56,846
	Feb 23	h	Division 1	Manchester United	1-0		52,544
	Feb 27	h	Division 1	West Bromwich Albion	3-3		35,940
	Mar 6	h	FA Cup	Colchester United	5-0	Ball, Kendall 2	53,028
	Mar 9	h	European Cup	Panathinaikos	1-1		46,047
	Mar 13	h	Division 1	Stoke City	2-0		38,924
	Mar 24	a	European Cup	Panathinaikos	0-0		25,000
	Mar 27	o	FA Cup	Liverpool	1-2	Ball	62,144
	Mar 30	h	Division 1	West Ham United	0-1		29,094
	Apr 10	h	Division 1	Wolverhampton Wanderers	1-2		35,484
	Apr 17	a	Division 1	Derby County	1-3		28,793
	Apr 24	h	Division 1	Blackpool	0-0		26,286
	May 1	a	Division 1	Crystal Palace	0-2		21,590
	Aug 24	h	Division 1	Chelsea	2-0	Harvey 2	38,854
	Aug 28	a	Division 1	West Ham United	0-1		26,878
	Nov 6	a	Division 1	Tottenham Hotspur	0-3		40,005
	Nov 13	h	Division 1	Liverpool	1-0		56,293
	Dec 4	h	Division 1	Stoke City	0-0		35,463

o *Old Trafford*   v *Villa Park*   w *Wembley Stadium*

Everton 3 Manchester United 1

August 19, 1967   Attendance: 61,452

Everton: West, Wright, Wilson, Kendall, Labone, Harvey, Young, Ball, Royle, Hurst, Morrissey

Scorers: Ball 2, Young

As Merseyside continued to rock the world, the Goodison congregation celebrated the union of 'The Golden Vision' and 'The Holy Trinity' as a blessing from above. Everton kicked off the new season against the reigning champions from Old Trafford and comprehensively trounced their star-studded visitors. The royal blue midfield trio out-thought and out-fought Charlton, Law and Best and dominated the proceedings with a display of breath-taking football. The demolition of Manchester United represented the first game in which the chemistry of Kendall, Harvey & Ball had gelled and the victory stimulated speculation of a possible challenge for the Division 1 title.

Michael Charters, *Liverpool Echo & Evening Express,* August 21, 1967

We have all been saying that this young Everton team will need a year or two to develop into a great combination, ripe to pluck the top football prizes off the tree. But by their superb display in crushing champions Manchester United 3-1 in the thrill-packed opener at Goodison Park, the boys in blue gave out the message quite clearly - 'we have arrived'. I'm sure no one at the club could have imagined that the team would show such maturity and command to thrash United as they did. I'm equally sure that it must be a long time since United were made to look such a stodgy outfit - out-paced, out-thought and out-played. Everton's performance was quite breath-taking, particularly in a 30-minute spell after the interval. United were reduced to a collection of disjointed units with indecision rampant, as Everton created gaps in the champions' defence with fast, intelligent and skilful attacking play. By contrast, Everton played magnificently as a team and brilliantly as individuals. Ball scored two goals by his unsurpassed ability to be in the right spot at the right time, moving up and down in constant, energy-sapping running, plus his skill in close dribbling and accurate passing. Labone and Hurst closed up the middle to erase any threat from Law and Kidd, while the midfield men, Kendall and Harvey, destroyed and created so well that they dominated.

Eric Todd, *The Guardian,* August 21, 1967

Everton overthrew them in a superbly contemptuous and disrespectful exhibition, the like of which we may not see again for a long time. The margin of victory 3-1 was almost irrelevant. I have no hesitation in suggesting that Everton are on the freehold of real greatness. They may not cross it this season or even next. But cross it they will. Against United, Everton revealed speed and precision, instinct and purpose. On an occasion as this when team work transcends everything, individual appraisal perhaps is unfair. Who, however, dare minimise the immaculate display of Wilson, the sheer brilliance of Kendall and Harvey, the artistry of Young, the industry and influence of Ball and the precocity of Royle?

David Meek, *Manchester Evening News,* August 21, 1967

Everton clattered United with more than three goals at Goodison Park. They rammed the realities of the new season well and truly home. Criticism of United must not detract from Everton's fine display. With Ball superb, they were very, very good.

Barry Davies, *The Times,* August 21, 1967

With six members of their team under 22, their potential is enormous and they will surely be one of the teams to beat. They also showed on Saturday, with Ball and Harvey leading the way, that efficiency and entertainment can go hand in hand, and their meeting with Tottenham Hotspur at White Hart Lane on Wednesday could add to the growing list of 'matches of the season'.

West Bromwich Albion 2 Everton 6

March 16, 1968   Attendance: 26,285

Everton: West, Wright, Wilson, Kendall, Labone, Hurst, Husband, Ball, Royle, Whittle, Morrissey

Scorers: Ball 4, Morrissey, Royle

'The Holy Trinity' had begun to hit their stride towards the end of the 67/68 campaign. With Colin Harvey sidelined, Catterick opted for an attacking 4-2-4 line-up with 17-year old Alan Whittle making his debut. Driven by Kendall and Ball in midfield, Everton produced one of their most emphatic away victories of all time and West Brom capitulated in the face of a near-ceaseless barrage. The result moved Catterick youngsters into seventh position in Division 1. However, the irony of this victory and the similarly one-sided 2-0 home triumph in October, was that Everton failed to win their most important contest against West Brom. At Wembley on May 18, both teams struggled through an unrewarding 90 minutes with the Blues squandering several goal-scoring opportunities. Inexplicably, they were beaten 0-1 in extra-time and their season ended in tears.

Horace Yates, *Liverpool Echo,* March 16, 1968

Everton took the lead in 23 minutes and Whittle played a big part in the move. He whipped the ball across to Husband, who headed forward into the penalty area. Ball ran on to it and hit a fine shot which Osborne had no hope of reaching. In 26 minutes Everton were two up and Ball again was the scorer. Whittle began the move by pushing the ball just inside the area and the international beat Osborne with a shot which was almost a replica of the first. After half-time Ball scored again to complete his hat-trick. Royle made the goal with a determined run in which he beat Colquhoun and Collard to earn a position inside the penalty area. On his way to goal he was promptly brought down. Ball scored from the spot. In 66 minutes Everton sailed into easy water. Morrissey beat the goalkeeper easily and again Everton were complete masters. The victory developed into a rout. Morrissey, from 30 yards out, crashed the ball against the bar and Royle was there to take over. Turning round quickly, he hammered a shot past the luckless Osborne. This was a devastating Everton. They were direct, effective and their finishing left nothing to be desired. Everton were playing as though they were enjoying every minute of the game. A crowd of youngsters invaded the field on 78 minutes to mob Ball on the scoring of his fourth goal, another penalty kick. It was awarded when Collard brought down Whittle. What a pity, I thought, that Everton had not allowed the youngster to take the kick to mark his debut with a goal.

Horace Yates, *Daily Post,* March 18, 1968

With what was probably the youngest team (fractionally over 22 years) ever to represent the club in a First Division match, Everton went to West Brom on Saturday and annihilated Albion. West Brom actually began the day two places above Everton in the League table, but it never looked remotely that way. With England team manager Sir Alf Ramsey looking on, Alan Ball scored four goals for the first time in his young life. Yet even his scoring extravaganza in no way stole the show from Alan Whittle, the youngest player on the field at 17 and sampling League football for the first time. To say that a player of Colin Harvey's talents was not missed is not a reflection on him, so much as a tribute to the team.

Horace Yates, *Liverpool Echo,* March 18, 1968

This was an easy victory only because Everton's superb play and marksmanship made it so. Everton served up a display on a par with that against Manchester United in the season's opening game and no team will live with Everton in this mood. While Ball scored four goals for the first time in his career, normally enough to earn any player star billing, he could not legitimately claim a greater share of the honours than Whittle.

Everton 7 Leicester City 1

November 30, 1968   Attendance: 42,492

Everton: West, Wright, Brown, Kendall, Labone, Harvey, Husband, Ball, Royle, Hurst, Humphreys

Scorers: Royle 3, Ball, Humphreys, Hurst, Husband

The Blues had enjoyed a brief spell at the top of the table in early-November and were determined to reclaim that position. Kendall, Harvey & Ball took a stranglehold on the game from the first-whistle and never relinquished it. They were rampant and out-classed Leicester by the speed, skill and endeavour of their midfield artistry. Although the home side were without Morrissey, his place on the left-flank being taken by young debutant Gerry Humphreys, they bombarded Peter Shilton in the visitor's goal throughout the game. The scoring extravaganza established Everton as the club with the highest tally of points in the history of the Football League and also sent a clear message that they were once again to be ranked alongside the best in British football.

Norman Wynne, *The People,* December 1, 1968

Everton lit up the murky atmosphere with an illuminating brilliance and leading the parade was hat-trick star Royle. He was robbed of an early goal only by a fantastic save from Shilton but he started the rot minutes later by running on to a Harvey pass to shoot home - and the massacre had begun. Ball who carved up Leicester with surgical skill, scored a second of such finesse that even Leicester applauded.

Mike Charters, *Liverpool Echo,* December 2, 1968

Leicester City came to Goodison Park on Saturday ripe for slaughter and Everton duly delivered the crunch with a display of the highest quality. Their 7-1 win was their biggest scoring spree since they beat Coventry City 8-3 on April 28, 1962 and it stamped them as the most attractive, entertaining team in the country. Statistical proof is impressive - 48 goals in 21 games; visual proof is there for all to see in the flowing skills of their attacking play. Everton were just out of this world at times with pace and precision which cut Leicester to ribbons. But the sustained play, the intelligent build-up, the remorseless pressure came from an Everton side operating smoothly on all cylinders with the super-charged drive coming from those marvellous men in the middle - Ball, Kendall and Harvey.

Horace Yates, *Daily Post,* December 2, 1968

The strolling maestros of Goodison Park, currently the most entertaining team in Britain, fulfiled the promise they have been parading for weeks, by slamming seven goals past labouring, luckless Leicester. One player does not make a team, but Ball has provided the flourish, the spark to light the flame and the example in match after match consistency that represents an irrefutable challenge to the rest. Undoubtedly Everton's greatest boon has been the bringing together of Ball, Harvey and Kendall to form the most lethal midfield trio of the present day. Their hallmark is stamped on almost every Everton accomplishment and they are young enough to keep Everton around the top for years.

RH Williams, *The Daily Telegraph,* December 2, 1968

Everton produced what in any other medium would have ranked as a lasting work of art. They were not even on television. Poor Leicester had no idea how to cope with Ball, who gets better and better but is merely the fulcrum of the team that seems certain to win the championship in a year or two, if not sooner. Ball brings his practice-ground tricks out playfully in the heat of the battle, but only because his mastery is so complete that he can afford a little showmanship. The straight men, Kendall and Harvey, were equally sure of themselves and the whole side seemed both correct and imaginative.

Everton 3 Leeds United 2

August 30, 1969   Attendance: 53,253
Everton: West, Wright, Wilson, Jackson, Labone, Harvey, Husband, Ball, Royle, Hurst, Morrissey
Scorers: Royle 2, Husband

Everton had strung together a series of impressive results, including wins over Manchester United both at home and away, and were confident of capturing at least on glittering prize by the end of the season. Leeds United were the ideal test of their new ambitions and arrived at Goodison with an unbeaten run of 34 League games. Although Tommy Jackson was required to deputise for the injured Kendall, the power and passion of the modified midfield overwhelmed the reigning champions. The star of the tremendous all-round performance was Johnny Morrissey, who enjoyed his finest royal blue outing by tearing the visitors' defence to shreds. For the most part Everton's football was spine-tingling and, in many respects, signalled the day that Catterick's young team came of age. The manner of the triumph proved to be their rights of passage into Goodison folklore.

Norman Wynne, *The People,* August 31, 1969
It's finally gone - that Leeds unbeaten record of 34 League games which began last October and took them to the League title. And who better to tame the champions than Everton, the pretenders to the throne? I am still trying to figure out how Leeds, so completely outplayed, could still put a respectable look on the scoreline. Praise Leeds for remembering they were champions in the final 20 minutes when a superb goal from Clarke raised an element of doubt about Everton's victory chances. But until then it had been Everton so far in front that one wondered how Leeds had gone unbeaten for so long. While Leeds carefully went into their well-rehearsed, slow-motion build-up, they had no-one with the flair of Ball or Harvey, and constantly ran into trouble in the compact Everton defence. The overall impression is that Everton are now ready to take over from Leeds - and they would be worthy of the accolade of champions.

Ronald O'Connor, *The Daily Telegraph,* September 1, 1969
Leeds United's record of 34 unbeaten games could hardly have been ended in a more brilliant match. Everton exposed the Leeds defence as has never been done before. In midfield there was little to choose between Ball and Harvey and Bremner and Giles, but where as Royle and Husband finished off the Everton pair's work with style and efficiency, the Leeds double-spearhead of Jones and Clarke were comfortably held by Labone and Hurst.

Horace Yates, *Daily Post,* September 1, 1969
This was a team performance of the highest order. Leeds were shattered at coming face to face with their masters. An elated Catterick said: *"They could not have been beaten by a better side."* Everton could be the team of the season, for playing as they are, not only are they a delight to watch, but their daintiness is merely an attractive cloak for the devastation they pack. Harvey and Bremner were set to cancel each other out - and nearly did. Paul Madeley was set as watch-dog on Ball and the fact that the Everton star was quieter than in any previous game is a tribute to a job well done, but it is also a tribute to Everton that with the brightest twinkling star subdued, the output all round was sufficient to produce this famous victory. Everton have cause for genuine joy and satisfaction. Husband's acceleration and elusiveness were a torment. Morrissey was a revelation and produced the finest football of his life. Charlton may be competing with Labone as the most talented of English centre-halves, but the fact remains he is no match for Joe Royle. He has savaged Charlton previously, but Saturday marked Joe's climb to the peak he has never scaled quite so impressively before. Not many modern players have the gift of making headers rival shots for power.

Liverpool 0 Everton 2

March 21, 1970   Attendance: 54,496

Everton: West, Wright, Brown, Kendall, Kenyon, Harvey, Whittle, Ball, Royle, Hurst, Morrissey

Scorers: Royle, Whittle

Try to imagine a special place that somehow crosses Nirvana, Xanadu and Utopia, well that was Anfield with Kendall, Harvey & Ball at their most elegant. The 102nd Merseyside derby witnessed a near-perfect performance by the royal blue midfield as their rapier-sharp passing game humbled Liverpool. With Ball captaining the team in the absence of Labone, the charge towards the championship heated up. The pivotal victory took Everton to the top of the table, some 11 points ahead of their red neighbours. Few football enthusiasts would have disputed that Kendall, Harvey & Ball ruled Merseyside and that Anfield had hosted their coronation.

Norman Wynne, *The People,* March 22, 1970
That League championship trophy is going to look good in the Everton boardroom next season - as good, in fact, as the kind of football the team is serving up on the way to winning England's premier trophy. For let no one doubt Everton's claim to being the best team in the land. Their football lit up a gloomy, rain-swept afternoon to make this one of the most exciting derbies of modern times as Liverpool put their trust in the old guard and recalled St John and Strong to work a one-game miracle. But it was a gamble which failed, as St John made little impact in midfield and Strong exposed to the speed and wiles of Whittle was booked for a vicious tackle on the little winger. The rest were often left gasping at the bewildering speed and beauty of an Everton attack built up on the skills of the best midfield trio in football - Ball, Kendall and Harvey - and finished by the deadly aerial ability of Royle. There was little Liverpool could do against a side which had no apparent weakness.

Max Marquis, *The Sunday Times,* March 22, 1970
Everton's revenge for their defeat by Liverpool at Goodison was unequivocal, complete and timely in the championship race. Nearly all of Everton's players did well but Ball, Harvey and Kendall were quite devastating. These were the firm triangular base for victory. Liverpool unhappily were a group of journeymen against the Everton artists.

Mike Charters, *Liverpool Echo,* March 23, 1970
No doubt about this cracking derby game. Everton won deservedly, gained ample revenge for their only home defeat this season, and their 2-0 Anfield triumph was gained with just as much authority as Liverpool had showed at Goodison last December. I was particularly impressed with the sheer professionalism of the performance. It was the day when their youngsters, Whittle, Kenyon and Royle, really blossomed in the frenzied atmosphere of derby day. There wasn't a weak link in the Everton ranks from back to front. But in the final analysis, it was the midfield where they took a grip and maintained their mastery, Ball spread his passes around with accurate initiative on a very heavy pitch. Kendall gave his best performance of the season in my book, with Harvey little behind him in workrate and effectiveness. The three of them picked up most of the loose balls in midfield, moved more quickly into the tackle and put Liverpool right out of their stride.

Denis Lowe, *The Daily Telegraph,* March 23, 1970
The return of Ball and Harvey and the recovery of their swift, skilful short-passing style has brought Everton four successive victories and made them look like champions again after all the doubts of mid-winter. Far quicker to the ball and more accurate and positive in its use, Everton had sufficient flair, imagination and teamwork to outweigh Liverpool's strong and eager running. Bill Shankly's latest formation involved the recall of St John to midfield, but in this department there was nothing the Scot, Livermore or even the formidable Hughes could do to compare with the skills of Ball, Kendall and Harvey, a purposeful and persevering trio.

Everton 5 Chelsea 2

March 28, 1970 **Attendance: 58,337**
Everton: West, Wright, Brown, Kendall, Kenyon, Harvey, Whittle, Ball, Royle, Hurst, Morrissey
Scorers: Royle 2, Ball, Kendall, Whittle

Billed as the climax of the battle for the championship, Kendall, Harvey & Ball and company went into the game as Division 1 leaders, after an unbeaten run of nine games, and slaughtered the FA Cup winners-to-be, who had only suffered two defeats in 31 games. The destruction was swift - a goal up in 14 seconds, 2-0 inside four minutes, 3-0 by the interval and 5-0 on the hour - and comprehensive. However the hero of the day was John Hurst, who received a bad cut to his head but played on wearing a skull cap. With Leeds losing at home to Southampton, The Mesrseyside Blues took a five-point lead at the top of Division 1 and remained unbeaten for the rest of the 1969/70 campaign. They were crowned champions for the seventh time on April 1 and finished with a tally of 66 points.

Eric Greenwood, *The People,* March 29, 1970
Elegant Everton can prepare to uncork the champagne. Given the tremendous fillip of two goals in the first three minutes, Everton ruled with an arrogant authority. The result was a one-sided romp by Royle and Co, superbly supported by the Ball-Kendall-Harvey dynamic trio.

Derek Hodgson, *The Daily Telegraph,* March 30, 1970
This was the superb Everton of last September, overwhelming opposition by speed and space. The Everton man on the ball almost always had two comrades running free and so could choose his angle of attack. Everton's victory was fashioned, if not in some Merseyside heaven, by the midfield trio of Kendall, Harvey and Ball, and any other national manager in the world would be happy to build his team around their near-divine football.

John Roberts, *Daily Express,* March 30, 1970
According to the official stop-watch of Everton's golden goal competition, Howard Kendall potted the ball in-off the far post in 14 seconds. According to majority opinion three minutes had elapsed when unmarked Alan Ball headed the second goal. From that point frustrated colleagues from the South writhed as Everton elegantly destroyed their London pride and joy 5-2. Catterick's team now play without pressure. They obviously enjoy being champions-elect.

Horace Yates, *Liverpool Echo,* March 30, 1970
"Champions, champions, champions." This exultant roar of acclaim for a feat still to be finalised, swept Goodison with a force of an explosion. Everton have long since exploded the theory that they are a fair weather side. Their fount of greatness undoubtedly was the control, creative skills and consummate artistry of the most talented midfield trio in football - Ball, Harvey and Kendall, for this was the occasion on which Harvey turned back the clock to something approaching his finest hours, enjoyed before his eye affliction took him out of the game.

Geoffrey Green, *The Times,* March 30, 1970
Everton have returned to the swaggering gait which earlier took them a street ahead of the field until the loss of Harvey with an eye infection and then Ball through suspension for a spell of 12 matches between November and February pulled them back. In this vein there is no more attractive side in England on their day. Inside the opening four minutes it was all over as Ball, Kendall, Harvey and company tore Chelsea to shreds. These three in midfield are the creative soul of this Everton side and together they proved themselves in perfect harmony again. In slanting rain and on a greasy surface where the ball moved liked lightning, they caught Chelsea on a day when they would have needed a couple of Bonettis and two or three Harrises to help them stem the tide. As Ball and his henchmen ran wild there was no one to plug the holes.

Alan Ball	player1966/67-71/72
Chris Beesley	*Ellesmere Port Pioneer*
Ian Bedford	*Chester Chronicle*
Stan Bentham	player 1935/36-48/49 & coach
Jon Berman	Everton fan, Liverpool
George Best	player, Manchester United & Northern Ireland
Billy Bingham	player 1960/61-62/63 & manager
Brian Birchall	Everton fan, New Brighton
Phil Bowker	Everton fan, Brussels, Belgium
Mike Brough	Everton fan, Bootle
Sandy Brown	player 1963/64-70/71
Mick Buckley	player 1971/72-77/78
Mike Burke	Everton fan, London
David Cairns	Everton fan, Newtonards, Co Down
Ian Callaghan	player, Liverpool & England
Tom Cannon	Everton fan, London
Len Capeling	*Daily Post*
Eddie Cavanagh	Everton fan, Liverpool
John Collings	Everton fan, London
Bobby Collins	player 1958/59-61/62
Mike Coville	Everton fan, New York, USA
Brendan Connolly	Everton fan, Frodsham
John Connolly	player 1971/72-75/76
Andy Clarke	Everton fan, Billericay
Ged Creighton	Everton fan, Liverpool
Norman Dainty	Everton fan, Liverpool
Frank D'arcy	player 1965/66-70/71
Terry Darracott	player 1967/68-78/79 & coach
Mark Denny	Everton fan, Wigan
Gerard Dingman	Everton fan, Liverpool
Steve Dingsdale	Everton fan, Whiston
Garry Doolan	*Daily Mail*
Bryan Doran	Everton fan, Liverpool
Tony Dove	Everton fan, Warrington
Eileen Downey	Everton fan, Prescot
John Dwyer	Everton fan, Liverpool
Paul Dwyer	Everton fan, Liverpool
Jim Emery	former-scout
David Evans	Everton fan, Lutterworth
Rick Fazackerley	Everton fan, Ormskirk
Wally Fielding	player 1945/46-58/59
Elizabeth France	Everton fan, Houston, USA
Jimmy Gabriel	player 1959/60-66/67 & coach
Chris Gill	*Daily Express*
Ronnie Goodlass	player 1975/76-77/78 & coach
Noel Gornell	Everton fan, Hightown
Andy Gray	player 1983/84-84/85
Claire Gray	*The Evertonian*
Peter Hackett	Everton fan, Kirkby
Brian Hall	player, Liverpool
Jackie Hamilton	Everton fan, Liverpool
Frank Hargreaves	Everton fan, Bootle
Brian Harris	player 1955/56-66/67
Colin Harvey	player 1963/64-74/75 & manager
Derek Hatton	Talk Radio
Charlie Hengler	Everton fan, Liverpool
Barry Hewitt	Everton fan, Colne
Dave Hickson	player 1951/52-55/56 & 57/58-59/60
Stephen Hickson	Everton fan, Carlisle
Ernie Horrigan	Everton fan, Liverpool
Norman Houncell	Everton fan, Liverpool
Mike Hughes	Radio Merseyside
Andy Hunter	*Daily Post*
John Hurst	player 1965/66-75/76 & coach
Jimmy Husband	player 1964/65-73/74
Stuart Imlach	former-coach
Tommy Jackson	player 1967/68-70/71
David Johnson	player 1970/71-72/73 & 82/83-83/84
Gary Jones	player 1970/71-75/76
Ronnie Jones	Everton fan, Liverpool
Tommy Jones	player 1950/51-61/62 & coach
Eric Jones	Everton fan, Hoylake
Francis Kane	Everton fan, London
Colm Kavanagh	Everton fan, Co Wicklow, Eire
John Keith	*Daily Express*
Howard Kendall	player 1967/68-1973/74 & 81/82 & manager
David Kennedy	Everton fan, Holmes Chapel
Michael Kenrick	Everton fan, Seattle, USA

Bill Kenwright	Everton fan, London
Roger Kenyon	player 67/68-78/79
Jim King	Everton fan, Liverpool
Brian Labone	player 1957/58-71/72
Gordon Lee	former-manager
Ed Loftus	Everton fan, Southport
Roger Long	Everton fan, Richmond
Joe Lloyden	Everton fan, Liverpool
Mike Lyons	player 1970/71-81/82
Ian MacDonald	Everton fan, Liverpool
John McAllister	Everton fan, Belfast
John McCormick	Everton fan, Bootle
John McFarlane	Everton fan, Skelmersdale
Sid McGuiness	former-groundsman
Duncan McKenzie	player 1976/77-77/78
Philip McNulty	*Liverpool Echo*
Jessie Milne	Everton fan, Liverpool
Steven Milne	Everton fan, Liverpool
Derek Mountfield	player 1982/83-87/88
Johnny Morrissey	player 1962/63-71/72
Alan Myers	Everton fan, Liverpool
Keith Newton	player 1969/70-71/72
Martin O'Boyle	*Speke From The Harbour*
John O'Brien	Everton fan, Liverpool
Denis O'Meara	Everton fan, Hightown
George Orr	Everton fan, Skelmersdale
Mike Owen	Everton fan, Liverpool
Phil Parker	Everton fan, Liverpool
Phil Pellow	*Satis?*
Mike Pender	Everton fan, Tarporley
Gary Pepper	Everton fan, Maghull
Fred Pickering	player 1963/64-66/67
David Prentice	*Liverpool Echo*
San Presland	Everton fan, New Brighton
John Quinn	Everton fan, Tewkesbury
Kevin Ratcliffe	player 1979/80-91/92
Phil Redmond	*When Skies Are Grey*
Paul Rigby	Everton fan, Connecticut, USA
Dave Roberts	Everton fan, Guildford
Ken Rogers	*Liverpool Echo*
Revd. Harry Ross	Everton fan, Ainsdale
Mike Royden	Everton fan, Great Sutton
Joe Royle	player 1965/66-74/75 & manager
Steve Seargeant	player 1971/72-77/78
Graeme Sharp	player 1979/80-90/91
Rob Sharratt	Everton fan, Narara, Australia
Neville Smith	Everton fan, London
Tommy Smith	player, Liverpool & England
Brian Snagg	Everton fan, Prescot
Mark Staniford	*Speke From The Harbour*
Trevor Steven	player 1983/84-88/89
Gary Stevens	player 1981/82-87/88
Ed Stewart	Everton fan, Bournemouth
Nobby Stiles	player, Manchester United & England
George Stuart	Everton fan, Lismore, Australia
Peter Stuart	Everton fan, Liverpool
Mark Tallentire	*The Guardian*
George Telfer	player 1973/74-80/81
Derek Temple	player 1955/56-67/68
Dave Tickner	Everton fan, Liverpool
Brian Tottey	Everton fan, Birkenhead
Glyn Tudor	Everton fan, Buckley
Tony Waiters	player, Blackpool & England
Mike Walls	Everton fan, Paris, France
Pete Warner	Everton fan, Chippenham
Gordon Watson	player 1936/37-48/49 & coach
Colin Watt	Everton fan, Cheadle Hulme
Fred Webb	Everton fan, Liverpool
Gordon West	player 61/62-72/73
Alan Whittle	player 1967/68-72/73
Billy Williams	Everton fan, Cologne, Germany
Alex Wilson	Everton fan, Liverpool
Graham Wilson	Everton fan, Ainsdale
Keith Wilson	Everton fan, Liverpool
Ray Wilson	player 1964/65-68/69
Neil Wolstenholme	Everton fan, London
Heather Woltz	Everton fan, Houston, USA
Tommy Wright	player 1964/65-72/73
Alex Young	player 1960/61-67/68